HARD WORDS... JUDGES FOR HARD TIMES

DR. C.Y. BISS

"Ponder the path of thy feet, and all thy ways shall be ordered aright" (Prov. iv. 26, *marg.)* is counsel for the child of God. These "Studies in the Book of Judges" may help to this end. They have been compiled from notes of addresses given by Dr. Biss, and are now published, with his kind consent, in the hope that they may prove useful to Bible Students. They will be most profitable if considered together with the passages referred to, which should always first prayerfully read. That growth in grace and knowledge, and power for happy service on the right lines may be the result, is the earnest desire of the Editor.

G.T. HUNT

Published by THE SOVEREIGN GRACE ADVENT TESTIMONY
1 Donald Way, Chelmsford, CM2 9JB Essex

About the Author

DR. CECIL YATES BISS was born at Calcutta in 1845, the son of godly parents, who were Strict Baptists. His grandfather was, indeed, one of the first Baptist missionaries in India, and a friend of William Carey. At an early age Mr. Biss went to New Zealand to join an elder brother. There, after the birth of their first son, he came to England in 1871. Mr. Biss became a scholar of Downing College, Cambridge, obtaining a first class in the Natural Science Tripos of 1875, and being appointed a Foundation Scholar as well as Winchester Prizeman. He took his B.A. degree in 1875; and was in the first class in the M.B. examination of 1880. In the same year he became a member of the Royal College of Surgeons, while he took his M.D. at Cambridge in 1884, and became a Fellow of the Royal College of Physicians in 1889.

His remarkable power as a preacher and exponent of the Word was recognized wherever he spoke, while his striking personality made him a power for good to all with whom he came into contact. When, on leaving Cambridge, he settled at Sydenham, he began, while busily engaged in his medical profession, a work at Wells Hall, which went on for some seven years. Preaching twice on Sundays, and on one evening in the week, he drew a congregation of those who loved and valued the Word of God as taught in its power and purity. The chief characteristic of his ministry was the gifted way in which he opened up the Scripture - not isolated passages, but whole portions or Books, going consecutively through whatever he began, word by word.

Ambassador Productions Ltd
Providence House
16 Hillview Avenue
Belfast BT5 6JR, UK.

Printed in the United Kingdom by Ambassador Productions Ltd.

The Book of Judges

is History—selected History—given with moral and spiritual objects. We must guard against wild analogies and distinguish between Types and Illustrations. The general character of the Book is to give Illustrations of Christian experience—Canaan being one of realised Christian position reached, enjoyed, used—and is made up of knowledge; facts and feelings. In

Ch. I. we have two opposite characters to consider. **Adonibezek.** vv. 5–7. **Achsah.** vv. 12–15. In Adonibezek we see God's principle of retribution. The time of retribution for Israel had come (*Gen. xv.* 18–21 *with ver.* 1). Note I. All things come under retribution, for God will bring every work into judgment; evil Agags as well as good Rechabites. II. That responsibility is proportionate to privilege. III. Retribution, being righteous, is fitted in each case to the actions to which it corresponds. *e.g.* (*a*) Trace how certain sins bring allied **consequences.** Selfishness degrades. Superficiality hardens. Impurity defiles. Carelessness deprives of worthy ideals. (*b*) Note the **forms** in which Retribution comes. The wealth of a life's gathering swept away in a day. Wisdom and learning of years perishing in a moment of paralysis. (*c*) Trace the **opposites** in virtues which bring blessings and blessings fitted to the virtues.

9–15. In Achsah we see woman's place and work. The characters in Scripture are always instructive. This ch. I is a chronicle of wars of large interests, yet in the midst of it we come upon a little family scene (*v.* 12). Kirjath-sepher really means a **city of books**; which, at a time when writing was in its infancy, was extraordinary and suggests it may have possessed a library! The dawn of the art of writing is as interesting as that of printing, and this city was of such importance that Caleb, the head of Israel then, made a promise in connection with the taking of it, that he would give his daughter to the conqueror of it. He knew not who would succeed, yet he made the promise and Achsah appreciated the honour of association in God's interests. It is certain God does bless nations and families according to the relation they maintain towards His Truth; *e.g.* see the special blessing to the Rechabites **on the earth** for obedience to their father (*Jer. xxxv.*)!

Achsah's mind was rightly exercised with the future position of Israel and she was willing to take him who should help towards it. She was a woman of faith in the **destinies of Israel** and rejoiced to be identified with one who could advance them. Her request was not a covetous one (*v.* 14). She desired a field that she might have a share in Emmanuel's Land, just as Naboth refused to give up his inheritance in it. Nor was her further request a worldly one. A south land is a dry land, so not a blessing without water; and Caleb treated her on the principle of "ask and ye shall receive, etc." We often don't ask because we don't desire; but Achsah came of good descent. Caleb had probably taught her well, so she asked rightly and intelligently; looking after her husband's interests at home.

Learn here to balance blessings rightly or we treat God's dealings in a one-sided way. The lesson of combination is difficult. "Upper and nether springs" are necessary or the balance will not be kept. We are often content that a south end should be watered to the neglect of the north. It is a humiliating lesson. Let us seek to read the Bible *as* God has given it us, and not magnify one portion to the detriment of others. It is easy to say this, but difficult to carry out. Achsah was thoughtful and prayerful; thinking of the needs of her inheritance.

The history of the Kenites.

16. Jethro was a Kenite, many of whom had thrown in their lot with Israel when they crossed the Jordan; and after Israel were settled, *they* settled in company with Judah in the wilderness. Now the Kenites are so often mentioned in Scripture, that it is needful to study their history.

The first reference to them as a nation is in a solemn passage among the doomed peoples of Canaan which God had so long spared, but which were to be cut off for their sins when their iniquity was come to the full—not before—so it was not an arbitrary act of God as some say (*see Gen. xv.* 19 *and Num. xxiv.* 22)! Balaam had mentioned Amalek as having special privileges (*v.* 20) which he had not used for God and the Kenites seemed to be strengthening themselves in evil; but in 1 Sam. xv. 6 we find Saul ordered them to " get out of the way " before he destroyed the Amalekites; which apparently shews they had drifted and gravitated back to their old Canaanite connections though delivered from destruction with them!

When Moses fled from Egypt he dwelt in the Midian desert with a priest, one of whose daughters he married. Though called " the priest of Midian " as dwelling there, he could not have been a Midianite as he is described as a Kenite (*v.* 16). He had wandered to the Midianites and was in a peculiar position as a priest and worshipper of the true God; serving Him by seeking to lead others to Him! Later on he brought his family to Moses, and hearing of God's wondrous works for Israel, he rejoiced and offered sacrifices to God! A remarkable fact! Here was a Gentile—one of a condemned nation—worshipping the true God; an instance of the distinguishing electing grace of God choosing and placing him in this prominent position; even above Moses and Aaron! In Num. x. 29 we find Jethro's son, Hobab, going with Moses and Aaron, and his seed cleaving to Israel at a time when they were a despised few; thus, putting themselves in alliance with Israel, they entered Canaan with them!

Again in Judges iv. we read of a special member of Heber the Kenite's family, who was yet further separated from his kindred and dwelling in the midst of Israel! In him there must have been some decisiveness as to the Truth of God and of Israel being His people, for it was his wife Jael—a Kenite—who destroyed Sisera, Israel's enemy! Not that the guile with which she entrapped him can be defended; but, evil as that was, there was a decision about her as to Israel, which led her to kill their enemy.

In 1 Sam. xxx. 29 they are found dwelling in cities; but

are not again mentioned until 2 Kings x. 15; where one Jehonadab is referred to. Jehu met this Jehonadab whose heart was right for God and helped to slay the worshippers of Baal! He must have been very decided against Baal and for God, for his mind was made up and he ready for action the moment he was called on!

In Jer. xxxv. the Rechabites are given by God as an object lesson to the Jews, in that they would not have a settled dwelling place nor drink wine in obedience to their father's command! God honoured them because they honoured their father. This is the last mention of the family, and it was at the darkest moment of Israel's history when these were here found **for God**! The Kenite nation was doomed to destruction, yet out of it was saved a remnant! They were a proud people, yet some were chosen by God out of them! All who are God's are His because He chose them; and there is no more forcible fact about "election" than the history of the Kenites.

Thus God chooses His people out of an evil world. The "grace" which dealt with the Kenites is the same which deals with sinners to-day. It is of God's mercy His people are where they are, and the Kenites' blessing shews that God always deals with "remnants" for **blessing.** In Rom. ix. St. Paul shews that the choice of Israel arose from God choosing Abram and Isaac and Jacob. So now, God has an "election" in Israel, and will bring them to **blessing.** It is blessèd to be one with God and one with His people as Jethro and the Kenite "remnant." When God gives "grace," we do choose Him and His ways and His people as Ruth; giving up other destinies for Him. And even if God's people go to the world for a time, they will eventually return; and it will be a blessèd thing to be with Christ and His people in Glory.

Now note the practical lessons. I. As God's people are an **elect** people, it is that they may be a **holy** people. They cannot accept the one and turn from the other. Holiness is separateness. There is no holiness without separateness. We would like to be like others. Our natural hearts go out to the world; but by "God's grace" we do **want** to be **holy and different from the world.** How can we be "lights" in the midst of darkness unless different from the people of the world? There should be distinctness marking us out from other people, or we shall be no use as "lights." We may be abused for it, but our life should speak as well as our words.

II. Holiness involves obedience. The Kenites were an obedient people to those who had a right to command them. This can be traced in every mention of them. There is nothing self-chosen in obedience; so holiness is obedience. They honoured the law of their father, and the Christian should not only obey God as God but as his Father; because God loves him as a father. Obedience should be yielded because it is his Father's law.

III. The Kenites were commanded not to dwell in cities but in tents. It would keep them from much evil. Jonadab would have been called a "Puritan" in these days; but it is true that the manners of the desert are purer than those of the city. So God's people should live in spirit and heart "outside man's city" as Abraham did. They would then be a heavenly people.

IV. The Kenites were to drink no wine. The world's wine of pleasure will wile God's people away from Him. If the love of the world is in them, the love of God is not. So consider what will make us care about God *and* what it is that is likely to make us careless about Him. What was God's purpose as to the Canaanites? 1 Sam. xv. shews that His wrath was against Amalek—one of the nations of Canaan—because of their sin. Some dare to call God's judgments on Agag a scandal! Such a thought would lead on to questioning His judgment at the Flood! Some judgments are executed in this life; some after death. They are a great deep and we may well tremble; but we must not slur them over. God spared the Canaanites 400 years, but His judgments at last fell on them. In Deut. vii. 1–5 we find God's directions were to utterly destroy them. His Word is very plain; so in slaying them, Israel did no more than does the executioner who puts a criminal to death. Israel was given no marginal discretion in the matter. See Ex. xxiii. 27–32, Josh. i. 1–16; and, as "all Scripture is written for our learning," this subject must necessarily contain lessons for us. Its spiritual interpretation is no mystery. It illustrates this; that in the Christian's experience are some positions of blessing which he cannot occupy till he gets rid of his spiritual foes; yet Israel's success was "the strength of God."

17. See the different way in which the various tribes dealt with the Canaanites. First Simeon. He went with Judah and destroyed Zephath, which was called Hormah *i.e.* "destruction;" and this is the brightest spot in the chapter, for they did precisely what God bid them—neither more nor less—the city and the inhabitants being **utterly** destroyed. They were "devoted to destruction," which marks how God deals with evil. So, where believers deal with sin root and branch, there is a Hormah and a place of blessing. Calvary proves that God hates our sins as much as He hated the Canaanites' sins, and there ought to be a conquest of sin in believers. They are not to live under its control.

18, 19. Next, Judah went west-ward alone and conquered the Philistines completely, God being with Judah. But how sad to find later on they returned to their cities and became quite at home in them! Thus sometimes, believers' victories are transitory. [There is no such thing as eradicating sin in this life. Though the believer gain victory over it, there is no deliverance here from its presence.] These heavy chariots, would be used in the valleys and Judah was powerless against them, yet God **could** have helped them. So we sometimes trust God to a certain extent and ourselves for the rest and thus only obtain partial spiritual success.

20. Hebron was a difficult place to take, but Caleb followed God fully, and though three Anakims were there, they fell like pigmies before God's strength!

21. There is a contrast here. The tribe of Benjamin did not drive out its Jebusite inhabitants, but made a truce with them—an unwholesome peace—perhaps thinking to improve them by association; and they remained there until David's time (2 *Sam. v.* 6, 7)! As oil and water will not mix, so never will good and evil amalgamate. Remember **this** any who make compromises! "What God hath put asunder let no man join" is as important as the reverse. Ch. xix. 10–12 and Josh. xv. 63 shew the evil of **this** compromise in what was to be "the Lord's city." The lesson

to be learnt here is, that there was something to be done in the Name and interests of God, *viz.* Jerusalem to be occupied; yet Israel failed to do it! Israel through all the times of the Judges was satisfied with only partial success. So in our conflicts with self, there is partial success and partial failure. Christians sometimes make terms with certain sins, but it is contrary to God's will and command. They cannot eradicate them but they should not be controlled by them.

22–26. Then Joseph; and the way his tribe went about this work was not creditable to them. He went not openly as Joshua against Jericho but with stealth and guile to take Bethel, and the victory was a humiliating one, for the betrayer went away and built a similar city elsewhere (*v.* 26).

27–32. In these verses are two examples of compromise. In the first it is assumed that **some** evil must be allowed; that it can't be helped. The Canaanites we read **would dwell among Manasseh**! Joshua would never have allowed it. The second compromise was with Asher, who **settled down among the Canaanites**; which was worse and gives a still stronger picture of a believer whose graces are so small, it is hard to recognise him as a believer.

34. Dan had a humbling experience. It was bad enough for the Canaanites to remain among Israel, but these Amorites forced Dan into the mountains; keeping the most fertile parts for themselves! Now this happens spiritually, when a believer does not take up a proper position with regard to his sin. If he try to do God's work in his own strength, he will have Dan's experience. The first condition for spiritual success against sin within is a right discernment of our **judicial** relation to it. "Holiness," as often taught now, forgets this, and much is said of Christ within, which may result in mysticism; and passages referring to legal relationship are applied to practical experience! A right apprehension of "Regeneration" is also necessary. It is too often regarded as the taming of our wild nature instead of as a new life created within. God wants no Canaanites in **His** works. Flesh is flesh not Spirit and is to perish presently. **Then** the new creation in us which is so feeble now will be more developed. "Holiness" must not be disjointed from Truth. There is no Pentecost or second Baptism of the

Spirit now, for God has given Him to **dwell** in believers, not as a visitor but never to leave them. His presence may be veiled that they cannot always realise this, but they may ask for a fresh measure of the Spirit. Israel failed because their faith failed. Once let a shadow of unbelief come in and the Canaanites will be victorious. Assurance of salvation is the **root** of "Holiness;" so keep fast hold of the promise "Him that cometh unto me, I will in no wise cast out."

Spiritual declension. Ch. II. contains four spiritual lessons; but let us first consider Israel's standing. They entered Canaan at Gilgal—the place of circumcision—thence to Bochim, where failure was announced and repentance needed: a place with a moral lesson for us. Israel were here commanded, as they had been over and over again, to have no association socially or religiously with the Canaanites. They were not only to manifest their own religion but to shew hostility to that of the Canaanites; and God helping them, to throw down their altars, etc. and not unite with them in friendship or marriage. If obedient, they would have a certain peace; but if not, the Canaanites would be as "pricks in their eyes and thorns in their side" (we know how painful even a grain of sand is to the eye), and their gods would ensnare and entrap them to terrible evil. There was something in the Canaanites' religion which would deceive and bring down God's judgment on them; the same as He intended for the Canaanites (*see Num. xxxiii.* 55, 56)!

We find here four lessons for us.

I. What the believer's relation to the world **is**: what it is **not** and what it **should be.** II. The certain blessings dependent on obedience. III. The nature of spiritual declension. IV. What believers' repentance is and how it differs from "repentance unto life" at the **beginning** of the Christian course. These are practical subjects requiring great grace; let us consider them as here illustrated.

I. The believer's relation to the world. We may not like and even refuse to admit the full claim of the truth that we are to have no association with the world. It is all around us; we are not yet in Heaven though in a place of certain blessing as Israel was, for they had means of grace from God to help them drive out the Canaanites. " The friendship of the world is enmity with God." It is a sphere in which Satan reigns—where the play of principles which come from " the pit " are set to work by Satan—so is it such that we can share its principles ; its work ; its objects or its pleasures ? God draws the line beyond which His people are not to go, but they are not willing to keep within that line. It is easy to make mistakes and difficult sometimes to see what we may or may not touch, so needful to consider these things walking in fellowship with God ; contrasting His principles with those of the world. Godliness and worldliness are positive things—not negative—and if heart and soul for God's things you will not be worldly. In I Cor. vii. 31 we find a principle to guide for all time. To " abuse " now means to act wrongly ; but the Greek word means to over use or use to the full. All in it must be used **for God**—friendships ; relationships, etc.—but not beyond that. May God save us from worldly relationships and religions !

II. Some blessings depend on obedience. God's dealings in Grace cannot supersede His dealings in Government. If He promise a thing on certain conditions, that is not Grace. God gave Canaan to Israel. That was of Grace ; but only if Israel drove out the Canaanites in God's promised strength would they possess the Land. Salvation is of Grace and of Grace alone ; for forgiveness is not deserved. But in Government, God **rules** and carries out His principles of Government ; and blessing follows obedience and punishment follows disobedience ; so then " Come out and be ye separate " saith the Lord, and " I will be a Father unto you ; " only on that condition. Contrast between God's forgiveness of sinners first coming to the Cross of Christ *and* His forgiveness of believers, which some fancy they have no need to ask for ! The first is based on Grace : but believers, realising how they ought to conduct themselves, find often they have grieved their **Father**—a **family** matter—and *must* pray " Forgive us our trespasses." In such cases it is the sin of **believers** ; needful to be recognised or they will be like Israel in the time of the Judges and incur God's chastisements because belonging to His family. Responsibility and chastisement belong to God's people. If they mix with the world, they become and remain as stunted trees, bearing very little fruit.

III. Spiritual declension. "Bochim" gives the character to this chapter. There is much spiritual declension among God's people. It is a gradual thing; an unperceived spiritual crumbling; not a sudden fall. It begins in the heart before it is seen in the life. Sc gradual was Israel's connection with the nations, that it was unperceived until God was as much against them as against the Canaanites (*v.* 14, 15)! Israel look as bad as the Canaanites and a fallen saint as a fallen sinner as far as this life is concerned, when God's hand is against him.

IV. Repentance in a believer is a change of mind. Man makes it a turning as to conduct but that is only partly true, for the conduct never alters until there is a change of mind. Repentance is only known by its effects. The tears shed at Bochim seemed deep; but feelings are delusive and often are merely sorrow for the effects of sin. The love of God produces true "Bochims" which are blessed. Do we mourn over our ways and carelessnesses? If not, we are in danger: so we do well to study this chapter.

Spiritual warfare. Ch. III. has a certain moral unity in its lessons. The first is obvious. (1–8.) It was Israel who spared the nations; but in another sense the Lord had left them, for Israel were not wishful to cast them out. Those left were five lords of the Philistines and the Canaanites among whom Israel dwelt. This gave them a changeful experience—one time up another down—a strong likeness to our own Christian experience in our struggle after holiness. The flesh, like the Canaanites, is left within to prove us; and we make peace with it until we find it taking possession of us and getting intolerable and seek the Lord for help. God knows us, but we need to know ourselves.

We have now the history of three men raised up to deliver Israel, and they did it in three different ways.

9–11. Othniel—an example of spiritual intelligence, who did a great work successfully and in a right way. Look at it in connection with the character of the principles he held. Not only did the Spirit come on Othniel but he also "judged Israel;" *i.e.* he put things right at home first. Here is a lesson for Christians of to-day who are tired of doctrine, and say "Let us go and convert the Chinese and take numberless versions of doctrine to do it with (*undenominational Societies*) *!*" There is indeed need of evangelising "regions beyond;" but missionaries must be rightly trained first or they will not succeed as Othniel did.

12—26. Ehud, on the contrary, sought to do the right thing but served God with wrong methods. He looked rightly on the Moabites who, though related to Israel, were their worst enemies; and he groaned over it. He could not overcome them by force and thought human skill should do it, so he resolved to use fraud and treachery! There was no need for this, for God Who raised him up could have enabled him to do what was a right thing in a right way. Thus Christians often seek to do good by wrong methods (*e.g.*, getting money from the world by bazaars, etc.). Seek rather to do God's work in God's way, and have no sympathy with Ehud's methods, though God's over-ruling providence allowed him to deliver Israel.

31. Notice now the faith and energy of Shamgar. Though a man of undeveloped faith, his "goad" was better than Ehud's "dagger." He was like a country clod apparently—not a trained soldier or a governor—but he felt God's enemies should be smitten and all he could find was an "ox-goad;" so what a terrible state Israel must have been in! Shamgar did not depend on means *or* despise them. He asked God to help him with his "goad" and with it he slew the Philistines! Learn from this that undeveloped methods may be successful if not wrong. An ungrammatical, faithful preacher of God's word is better than a refined one, if unscriptural.

Now the first question to be settled by every Christian is his relation to Faith and the relation of Faith to him. He fancies in his first experience that a course of unalloyed joy is before him; but his first lesson will be to learn the unprofitableness and evil of his own heart—a humbling one. We say "we are evil" far more than we believe it and we think we improve; but it is not so. The flesh cannot be **improved.** The Canaanites never became Israelites and

Israel were not to try and assimilate themselves to them but to keep separate. Even if a Canaanitish family appeared nice, they were not to seek to ameliorate them. All efforts to improve the flesh come to nought; the devil is sure to triumph (*v.* 6)! And the flesh cannot be **ignored.** Some think it can be abolished; stunned; arrested in its power for evil, but that is not a Scriptural thought: there will never come a time when the believer will not be conscious of the presence of the law of evil within. If the flesh is a fact in human experience, it is not safe to ignore it. It was better for Israel to see the Canaanites than to ignore them. Let a Christian say "I've got a victory over the flesh" and he will soon find himself under its power.

Notice in this chapter, God never works deliverance for Israel apart from them but with them; giving them strength against their enemies and they striving as if alone. They were not automata or set aside as at Jericho. They were being trained by God, and at their worst were better than the Canaanites at best. It is an important lesson for us; *viz.*, to rely on God's strength and at the same time to go and fight the battle; otherwise it is no use talking of "consecration" and "abiding in Christ."

Ch. IV. Faith in Action. Compare ver. 2 with Josh. xi. 1–13. "Hazor" must have been rebuilt and the few people left so multiplied, as to be able to oppose Israel with a formidable force and keep them in subjection! "Jabin" may be taken as the name of the Head of the dynasty; as Abimelech, Pharaoh, etc.; so that men's sneers at the inaccuracy of Scripture are quite beside the mark.

I would take this as an illustration of an important spiritual lesson; *viz.*, that the flesh never dies. Our enemies are never exterminated. They may by God's grace be kept under control, but the Jabins and Hazors of our souls are ever ready to spring up and do the old work in their old vigour. God's strength alone is sufficient to overcome our enemies, and a fresh application by faith to **that** is needed each day to enable us to overcome them. True, God uses our experiences and habits to that end; but do not lean upon them or you will surely fall,

We have here three examples of **Faith in exercise** from different points of view.

I. Deborah—a very perfect example. She was the first woman who "judged Israel." Women in Scripture are not put into prominent places of ruling except in days of failure, and these were days of peculiar defection; more so than in the days of Ehud and Shamgar. They had almost lost even the knowledge of God, and God marked the condition of those times by raising up a woman to rule! He shewed their wisdom and resource were not to be found in the wisdom and strength of the instrument. There is no revelation now; no prophetic ministry as in 1 Cor. xiv. 6—33; the object of which was "to exhortation, edification and comfort (*v.* 3)." This prophetic ministry was sorely needed in Deborah's time; and what do we need now? We need a ministry to guide and instruct; to expound the prophets—exposition that shall be heart-moving, not sentimental—shewing their meaning. Yet how little there is of such ministry! Deborah-like ministry we do need. I beseech you to pray for it; though when I speak of Deborah-like ministry, I do not mean public preaching by women, but Priscilla-like teaching of God's Truth. You may say "Why do we need it? Can we not read our Bibles and study at home?" But God's plan is to have Truth expounded as by Ezra (*Neh. viii.* 8), and by Philip, who took the Book from the eunuch's hand and explained its meaning; and He gave "teachers" to this end.

II. Barak—a very imperfect example. He is mentioned in Heb. xi.; but notice the place his name occupies; not first in order of time, for the order must be moral and significant as to the display of the Faith exercised by these worthies. Gideon's was superior to Barak's, and probably David is mentioned before Samuel for the same reason. Though Barak's faith was inferior to Gideon's, still he is there; but his story is a mingled one. He may have argued that Deborah, being better known, would be the proper one to take the lead; but, when called again he trembles no longer and God gave a wondrous victory (*v.* 6–15). Barak was an example of Faith; not of great Faith but of Faith marred by unbelief. Nothing is said in Heb. xi. of Deborah's faith but Barak's is noticed: yet note, that his faith being incomplete, his work was incomplete. His reward was lacking (*v.* 9); as much as to say "You will not have the honour you might have had!"

Similar examples are found in the New Testament (*Col. iv.* 17, 2 *John* 8, *Rev. iii.* 11). "Blind unbelief is sure to err." Right work is the effect of right Faith. God's way was the way for Barak, but he hesitated and God sold his enemy into the hand of a woman! Jael's nail not Barak's sword was the instrument of Sisera's death! "Them that honour Me I will honour." Do your work Christians, in God's way and you shall have God's reward. Don't do His work on man's principles.

III. Jael—who had Faith but put it into action in a wrong way. The lessons to be learnt from her are Barak's over again, but failure is more crudely revealed. Remember she did not know of the defeat that had taken place; so think of the tremendous risk she ran! She knew by Faith that God **would** give the victory and that Sisera was His enemy and must accordingly perish, therefore she acted as she did. But was she therefore a murderer? Was Samuel a murderer when he "hewed Agag in pieces before the Lord?" Was it wrong? Is there no such thing as retributive justice? Do men argue thus when justice overtakes a murderer? It is only when they want to find fault with God's Word that they make an outcry like that. Would it have been wrong had Barak's sword killed this wicked oppressor? So was it wrong that Jael's nail did? No! but the deceit was wrong. Rahab was not wrong to hide the spies, but she was to tell a lie about it. Deceit of heart mingled with Jael's faith in God; and we too dishonour Him when we do His work in our own way.

Ch. V. Deborah's Song is one specially for believers, in which **reasons** are given for **the success or failure of individuals in the work of God.** It is an inspired song; and Barak is associated therewith though he spake not a word of it. He had retired from the post of honour that he might have had had his heart been whole and his eye single. It is Deborah who says again and again "I sing;" "I arose, etc." God spoke to His people of old through the lips of those whose voice was for the moment the voice of Prophecy and which said "Hear ye the words of the Lord (*v.* 3)." These either took the form of address, parable, prayer or song. In Hebrew a spiritual song means an inspired song and to sing in the Spirit means under the influence of the Spirit. A fallen Church cannot speak now as in 1 Cor. xiv. We cannot say ver. 15 now; but Paul's words referred to such an inspired Song as this, which carries on it the stamp of Divinity. They are not Deborah's words but God's, whether of curse or blessing. Men speak of the prophets as "clever men with a great insight" but it is a false idea. Deborah may even have been an ignorant woman. It was the Grace of God made her what she was.

6. "In the days of Shamgar and Jael the highways were unoccupied" for fear of the foe! It is clear from the way Jael is mentioned that she was the wife of that Heber who slew the enemy near Kishon. It is possible that she and her husband lived in the south near Shamgar formerly (*iii.* 31) and that later on they moved their tent up near Kishon. Possibly she had been in some way an instrument of blessing to Israel, and v. 6 shews she did not come to the front for the first time when she slew Sisera.

7. Instead of settling together in villages, Israel scattered themselves to avoid being an attraction to the spoilers "until Deborah arose a mother in Israel." A mother is better than no parent, but yet not so good as a father; and Deborah assumes no higher position than that of "mother," yet she set Barak on his feet!

8. Here is the source of Israel's misery—"They chose new gods"— turning their back on the true God! They were at war, but no weapon amongst them; so helpless were they before the forty thousand of the foe!

9. Great courage was needed at such a time to make a stand against these and Deborah's heart ran out to those who were willing to do so . . . . Christians do not serve God so truly when they have a position to maintain or wealth to engross them. It is a blessèd thing that some "wise" and "noble" do. The Grace of God is at the bottom of all right movements.

10. "Riders on white asses" were prominent members of society. Ver. 11 means that Satan keeps souls from the streams of Truth; but those who succeed will record God's deliverances.

12–13. Barak led captive those that had been leading captive.

14–22. Deborah recapitulates all she had learnt going in and out among the people. Some were half-hearted; being content so long as they were left to a prosperous quiet life. A few in Ephraim were standing against Amalek; and in Benjamin, Manasseh and Zebulun there was a certain devotedness to God in individuals. But Reuben had forgotten God and debated whether it would be better to serve the enemy or resist him! He should not **at that time** have "abode among the sheep folds;" and for Dan to "remain safely in his ships" shews he had no love for his brethren in Israel *or* for the God of Israel! There were few like Zebulun and Naphtali who "jeoparded their lives unto the death"—seeking God's interests first.

23, 24. Notice here the "curse" of Meroz and the "blessing" of Jael; they contain lessons for all time. No place can now be identified as Meroz. That is unnecessary; but when its people were called to help towards God's cause they refused! It was a negative rather than a positive sin. Some now who are unconverted boast and delight in **neutrality.** It gives less trouble and they call it their religion. They are not atheists, but like Meroz, they do nothing. They do not want to know the Truth; arguing, that "as one says one thing and another another, how are they to know what is right?" instead of taking the trouble to find out from Scripture. It is a despicable thing to say "I don't join anyone;" so remember the curse of Meroz. You must either love *or* hate Christ, for not to love is to hate. Ponder on 1 Cor. xvi. 22, "If any man love not the Lord Jesus Christ let him be accursèd **when** the Lord cometh!" The curse of Meroz lies on such, and it stretches on to the coming of the Lord and to Eternity!

Among Christians too, are some who confuse earnestness with fanaticism; but read Christ's words to the Laodiceans. Does He like lukewarmness? Why do you go on without making sure what is right? Being a resolute follower of Christ is not being a fanatic. Each one should ask himself whether he is with God's people or with the world. The people of Meroz were not in earnest. They only begged to be let alone; but if these truths are from God, they do concern one and all. Some are like Meroz as regards work for the Lord while there is much around waiting to be done. All God's servants are called to serve *now*. Have you a work for God every day like you have in earthly things? You know what your work in life is; so you should your work for God. All are called to do something and not be idle. There is a curse on spiritual inactivity which brings spiritual disease. The soul gets dulled and all interest in Divine things dies out. So be earnest and active; not neutral and selfish. You must be either with Christ or against Him.

24. Jael was not like Meroz, yet not perfect. She had no right to tell a lie but she was right to kill Sisera, though she should have done it in a right way.

Gideon. Ch. VI. commences with the history of a "man of God;" recounting his deeds of faith in much detail. Three chapters are devoted to him, while a few verses suffice for Barak. Both were men of faith and mentioned in Heb. xi., but what a difference in their faith and its developments!

1. An interval of forty years had been long enough for another generation to grow up and for God's deeds for Israel to be forgotten. Canaan was a fertile land and Israel must have been prosperous or the Amalekites would have had no inducement to come down on them. But these years of prosperity had been years of forgetfulness of God! It was the tendency of Israel to forget God and to fall away from Him. We are not told the details of this declension, but probably it was occasioned thus. The Canaanites had remained and intercourse had gone on doubtless at markets; in social life; by intermarriages and at religious festivals; though Moses had forbidden attendance at heathen feasts lest they should be induced to eat of idolatrous sacrifices (*Ex. xxxiv.* 15); but Israel soon lost this thought of separation

and they became weak! Mark the lesson on this, that the noblest instances of men are developed only in connection with the knowledge of God. Be sure that if this country goes on in theosophy, evolution, agnosticism and the like, as it is going, it will be very different country from what it should be. England has been singular in her righteousness though she has had her sins; but she has had the Bible and acted on its principles. If she gives them up, she will fail as did Israel! Forty years in the times of the Judges did it for Israel (*ch. v.* 31), and chastisement came to them from the "Midianites and Amalekites and the children of the East."

Notice that on this occasion their chastisers were their kindred. Midian was Abraham's son by Keturah and Amalek of Esau's family, but both alien from God and from Israel's promises. So in the believer's experience. The greatest foe is in his own household. He has to groan over the evils of his own heart; over the elements of his own self. His lusts and selfishness say "Indulge me." The old nature—the old Adam—is in him, but there is also the new nature—the new man—and the conflict between these is like the scene here. "The flesh lusteth against the Spirit and these are contrary one to the other." Which shall succeed? The voice of the Holy Spirit listened to, turns the tide, and the moment God appears there is victory over the foe. When God is in their midst, a company of 300 is more than sufficient (*ch. vii.*)! Our worst foes are not the Philistines. There is nothing so humbling and profitable as the lesson that "in the flesh dwelleth no good thing."

These foes of Israel had all the good of the land from the rich valley of Esdraelon down to the south, so that at harvest time it was sad to contemplate the waste of this fertility. In like manner the harvest of the soul can be swallowed up by the evil in ourselves. But blessing came to Israel in the old way by God giving them grace to feel their need. A simple lesson. The soul needs instruction. Unless it knows its poverty, it will not seek blessing and go to Christ. We sometimes wish we could feel our sin more so as to sorrow rightly for it; but let us just leave our souls in God's hands, believing Christ's words "Him that cometh unto Me I will in no wise cast out."

8. God sent Israel a prophet first—not a deliverer—to shew them "whence they had fallen." We are only told his "message," not if he even saw Gideon; but we find that those who **helped him** were **prepared** for their work evidently by the ministry of this prophet. This is the kind of ministry the Church needs now; for the Church, by such things as evolution and the like which have swept over our land and blotted out the Bible, is suffering the present blight. What do we hear all around but that the state of the Church is one of starvation; and even if the truths of Scripture *are* taught they are adulterated with error! *e.g.*, Prophecy is mixed too often with the unscriptural thought of the "Secret rapture" which brings a blight. We need a ministry conducted on the lines of the ministry of this prophet, which was doubtless very conventional in style and his sermons must have been conversational and to small gatherings. Oh! if those who know the Truth would only minister it in that way—by personal intercourse; little meetings; conversations etc.—and not be selfish!

Gideon's work may have possibly begun in his own soul through the ministry of this prophet! He is introduced to us suddenly, but in a way which shews his heart was right. He was found in very humiliating work; threshing a handful of wheat in a winepress—not a threshing floor—where the Midianites would not expect to find him; without a flail and not daring to do it in the light of day! There the Lord manifested Himself to him in the form of an angel (11–16)! That it **was** the Lord is proved by Gideon not being reproved when he worshipped Him; and the announcement "The Lord is with thee, thou mighty man" could only have been assured him by God. Gideon was scarcely prepared for this (*v.* 13). Faith has its puzzles and is often allowed to have them.

Now for the application. Remember, if we are God's believing servants and have some conception of the present sorrowful hour and some knowledge of how God's Truth is devastated, then there is something for God to work upon as in Gideon. Not as prominently as in him, but silently and quietly. Then He may bless. We here see how God called and **prepared** Gideon for the work of delivering Israel. In previous instances of raising up "saviours" for Israel, their **work** is given but less of their **preparation** for it. But in Gideon—this man of great faith and mentioned as such in Heb. xi.,—we are led to consider the nature of his "call." It is suggested though not mentioned, that Gideon had come under the power of the prophet's ministry (8–10) ; a ministry similar to John Baptist's, leading to repentance and what the "two witnesses'" in Rev. xi. *will be*, of wrath to come on Jerusalem but with no message of grace, for the Gospel will at that moment have been withdrawn from Jerusalem.

So here ; a feeling of need must come before the message of grace is given. Gideon had been prepared for work under this ministry as seen by the character of his answer (*v.* 13). His heart had been exercised about the Midianites causing widespread misery, and wondered if God were the "God of **Israel**," why it was thus. Experienced hearts are often ignorant hearts as Gideon's was of Deut. xxxi. 17. He was awakened, but unenlightened as to Israel's sin being the cause of their circumstances and of God's withdrawal. When God begins a work in the soul He continues it ; so we come to His communication to Gideon (*v.* 14). Notice what an instance of Grace it was, not only in a social sense—Gideon's family being so small—but also in dealing at all with Israel at this time, when there is no evidence that any single one had sought Him. Yet miserable as Israel then was, God came to them in Grace ; and the same is true of individuals, to whom in their darkest hour God has come ; stopping their mad career ; displaying Himself in the Cross of His Son and not requiring anything. Pure Grace brings God to Israel and Israel to God ; for God turns to us before we turn to Him. No sheep ever seeks the shepherd ; it is the shepherd seeks the sheep. None of themselves "understand or seek after God." Does anyone desire to be one of God's sheep for ever ? If there be the yearning, remember Jesus says "No man can come to Me except the Father . . . draw him ;" and "Him that cometh unto Me I will in no wise cast out."

Did Gideon **deserve** that God should turn to him ? But this is the character of Grace ; just as the prodigal's father ran to meet him. God's commission to Gideon was "Go in this **thy** might !" What constituted the might ? The fact that God had sent him and **He** never makes a mistake and sends the wrong one. So Gideon could be **sure** God had sent him; and more, that He would be at his side at all moments. Yet later on (*v.* 17) he asks for a sign! But do not be hard on him, for his is the experience of most Christians when they ask for **evidence** that God's promises are true. There is an analogy between Gideon's case and our own. God calls; His strength lies in the compass of His call and His declarations are promises. See Ezek. iii. 4–15. As soon as the prophet began to go he heard the rushing of the agencies of the Spirit; all Heaven going with him to make him successful! But that is equally true of you and me anywhere, if we accept God's call and commission. If **He** send us to work, we shall not be at a loss for the means; therefore let it never be said "**How can** it be done?" or "I can't do it," as Moses said and lost the honour God intended for him; Aaron being sent to aid him! *Our* might still consists in two facts—"I have sent thee" and "I will be with thee (14, 16)"—though there is such a thing as running before being sent; and there may be something in our ways which hinders God going with us. Gideon apprehended the great fundamental truth *viz.*—"they shall be all taught of God." A man must **feel his need** before he can understand the Gospel. The Gospel is not a mere civilizing; a thing that can be explained to everybody. Conviction of sin and need of pardon are necessary and must be felt by the soul.

17, 18. It was remarkable he should ask for a sign; but he seems to have had an apprehension of the fact that "Sacrifice" is the basis of a right relation to God. He felt that if there were to be this communion of work with God, there must be an "offering"—a meat offering (*see marg.*)—which is as much sin-purging as the Burnt Offering. There were not only "unleavened cakes" but a "lamb slain;" thus interposing a **sacrificed life** between himself and God to put a cover on the offerer *and* to be accepted for him. Then he waits for it to be taken, which the angel did in a way characteristically Divine; touching it with His staff which brought fire to kindle it (21)! The "broth" poured out on the "sacrifice" illustrated Israel's poverty-stricken condition.

23, 24. Notice again, that "peace" came to Gideon before he entered on service. Gideon's first thought was that he must perish because he had seen God. There was deep conviction of sin in him, and he felt it was not fitting for his sinful self to be so near to God. He was just beginning to feel how bad and evil he had been and thought he **must** perish; but it was the very opposite, for though he deserved to die—having been a Baal worshipper—yet "sacrifice" had been accepted **for him** in the slain kid, and the Lord said "Peace be unto thee." Then Gideon erected an altar there, calling it **Jehovah-Shalom,** *i.e.* "The Lord send peace."

The lesson here is this. Is there any one who cannot say "Jehovah is my peace?" Then you have not sought peace in the right place. You have sought it in your own self and heart instead of outside you, in God. "We have an altar" greater than Gideon's—even Christ and His worthiness—so lean upon His finished work for peace.

> **"I hear the words of love; I rest upon the Blood;**
> **I see the mighty Sacrifice; And I have peace with God."**

25–40. In attempting to bring out the subject outline of this passage we will consider it under two divisions. I. **Gideon's personal circumstances.** II. **His growth in Grace and preparation for service.** As soon as Gideon had taken hold on the fact that "peace with God" had been established by Sacrifice, he was called to the most trying experience. On the mount where Baal had been worshipped, Jehovah was to be acknowledged and the bullock sacrificed! The wood to be used was the wood of the "grove" (*lit. image or statue of Astarte*), which was to be cut down! The lesson for us here is, that the service of God's people begins at home; in one's own experience and circumstances. The work of God is not like a wave coming over us, but rather as a ripple on the water caused by casting in a stone. The circles become wider and wider, but the ripple begins from within. All true work begins in a man's own soul. Man is what comes out at home and the work that begins there is far more difficult. Jehu could point to his "zeal for the Lord" while his own sins were unsubdued. This is a much needed lesson. If desirous of serving God are we willing to begin with self? Gideon's was a bold and perilous work, as is shewn in the phrase " because he could not do it by day he did it by night (*v.* 27) ! " There was danger at home—from " his father's household "—and also from " the men of the city ; " but the dangers connected with work kindle the daring that dares the danger ; and danger and difficulty make us feel our own weakness and drive us to God to be strengthened with His might. Gideon did not say " I am called to this work and I cannot do it ; " but what he could not do by day he did by night ! Let us learn the lesson of his spirit concerning devotion of heart ! "True, I may not be able to do it **thus** or **now** ; but do it I will." God always blesses the " counsels of the heart " in His service. Gideon's work is not given to us, but work is given. Does it not succeed ? It may not have been begun in earnest, or we have grown weary in the doing. Gideon's was not done in his natural strength but was the working of grace in his life. He was no fanatic. He did not seize a hammer and rush off and demolish the altar ; he did it in the spirit of 2 Tim. i. 7.

Notice again how the Grace of God working in Gideon differentiated the men around him. His kinsmen were **in** the existing state of things, and if left to themselves would have been ready to kill him ; but, when the critical moment came ; when the die was cast and it was a question on which side they would stand ; they came out on Gideon's side (*v.* 31) ! and, when the " men of the city gathered against him they found, not Gideon alone, but the men of his house prepared to defend him ! **We** may be saying " what deliverance can **we** work ? " Be faithful and bold. God can make you the test of some who will take their stand for God and His Truth (2 *Cor. ii.* 15, 16).

31, 32. This is an interesting incident. The name **Jerub-baal** was not given him by his father but came to him in a much more natural way. Men called him **what he was.** When he took his stand on God's side they then saw a man who brought Baal's cause to the test and **in consequence** called him **Jerub-baal.** It was a name of honour. Such a moment may not come to us, but when I read in Revelation the mention of a " new name," I see in **that** an intimation of the truth that God has names for His people in connection with their service here. It will be one that will bring sweet reminiscences of what was wrought in our hearts and lives by His grace. "Thou hast been faithful over a few things, I will make thee ruler over many things." The future must by God's providence be somehow woven into the threads of the present; or at any rate, be an extension of the present.

II. **Gideon's growth in Grace.** There are two circumstances which shew how God caused Grace to grow in Gideon's heart. Our first reflection is this. God **knows** His people. He made the heart and therefore **knows** it and that all are not alike; so He does not deal with them alike. Peter was not like John nor Philip like Thomas: neither was their unbelief like that of Judas. All these instances shew that God knows how to deal with each according to their different character. We do not understand many things that we see and wonder at in others, but God understands, and if we could measure ourselves as we measure others, we should see how different we appear to them to what we do to ourselves. God adapts His gracious dealings to each as He sees their need. Gideon was not timorous as Timothy, but he was very much afraid of making mistakes. He knew God had called him to this work, but wanted to make sure that he was doing it in the right—the Divine way—and also in God's time. God alone knows how feeble we are and how tenderly He feels for us. When too weak we are taken up and carried (*Is. xlvi.* 4); and here Gideon was questioning whether the circumstances had come in which he was to act, to be assured that all was right (*v.* 37).

38–40. See how God loves Faith; so when cast down remember this fleece. God's patience made the miracle the more remarkable. When Gideon asked that the **fleece only** might be wet, he might think this to be more in accordance with nature than the opposite condition, so he requested a further proof, by asking that the dew might be on the **ground only**; and God graciously answered his petition. So with Hezekiah (2 *Kings xx.*). Oh! the tenderness of God! Be not afraid to trust Him. The second circumstance is in

Ch. VII., where we have another wonderful lesson. Gideon had not been quite sure if the right moment had come to start with his little band of men, but now God takes the initiative and we learn that God's work for His people is so wrought, that two ends are obtained. First; His own glory. Secondly; the education, training and discipline of His people. Why did not God put Midian to flight in a moment? He **could** have done so and **has** sometimes without man's instrumentality! But here He would not work without Israel, for He takes pleasure in His people. **We** may argue "Why could not God give us deliverance from our foes more promptly and in other ways?" Because He has **His** purposes in view; *viz.* the education of our souls. We are also to "work out our salvation;" not work *for* it but reduce it to practice and detail with earnestness and intensity of feeling—not allowing it to remain as a principle dormant in the heart—yet "with fear and trembling." God designs certain ends *in* us for **His own** glory and *through* us for **our interests**; so we are not automata. God uses us as thinking, feeling beings; accomplishing something in us, in association with Himself. Therefore "work," remembering the presence of our God; and "in fear;" not lest you should not get to Heaven, but, as Moses when he put off his shoes from his feet being on holy ground, "work out" God's design in your lives. God would not deliver Israel from the Midianites without them, yet in such a way that it should be **seen it was** God's arm that gained the victory.

2, 3. We see the abstention of several tribes; and even of the army selected from Israelites in the north, only a small portion was to be used! Had many been employed the victory would have been attributed to their skill and power; so two-thirds returned.

3. Now notice God's work and principles connected with those who were chosen. 1st **Separation.** 2nd **Courage.** 32,000 offered themselves for the work but 22,000 were not suitable! Separateness is necessary in all work for God. If God's servant is not willing to leave all he is not fit for God's work. Matthew "**left all** and followed Jesus!" God's "call" is above all earthly work and interests. Until we admit we are not acting or working on earthly principles we are not even like the 10,000 who were willing to work for God. Are we prepared to stand out from the bulk of

men and on the side of Christ and His principles ? Among those who had the **separateness**, the greater part had not the needed **courage** ; as John Mark, who had not faith to go on but left the Apostles in their hour of need and went home ! It did not make him not a Christian and the words "looking back from the plough" are not applicable in his case. He was not prepared to go all the length which the work of Paul demanded ; but later on we find him prepared for the work of the kingdom of God, though even *then* he was **in it** as regards his soul's salvation. So now, some Christians stick in the mud like John Mark. You like to hear gospel sermons ; but are you always going to be a baby and never a man ; a worker ? There are deterrent circumstances may be, and it is needful for you to seek what it is that keeps you back from being an out-and-out Christian—a devoted servant of Christ—without fear ! Ask God to take away your cowardice.

4. Here we get a further lesson. We have a process of education which has a three-sided bearing. Each one is instructed for himself, and one is not to judge another but to be tender with God's other servants. We judge others when we begin to talk of their **motives.** St. Paul did not speak of John Mark's **motives.** It is imperfect understandings which lead to imperfect judgments among God's people. . . . On the other hand there is sometimes a temptation to abstain from interfering when one can and ought to. Now why were 300 chosen to go with Gideon and no more ? The army was going to battle ; and Gideon led the men to the well of trembling and we may infer he encouraged them to drink of the water to refresh them for the war. And these 10,000 were found to drink in two different ways. All but 300 drank in a leisurely way—"going on their knees to drink." Worldly men would argue that they were sensible and thoughtful. But how different are God's ways from man's! He saw by their way of drinking that they were unfit for this work. They were "using His blessings to the full," whereas the 300 just took as much as their hands would hold, making that sufficient for their present need and rushed forward. Not stopping to kneel, they were ready before the rest and were in the front rank. They had separated themselves and

God had separated them, so that they were ready in an instant for action while the rest were unprepared.

Let us see the lessons here. Small circumstances often declare great issues. A straw on the stream shews the way of the tide. Insignificant events shew the moral current of lives—a test as to wholly devoted or partly devoted ones. Are there none such in our own ? Little calls of duty ; tests of patience, etc. ? If the world **in a body** were to ask us to apostatize from Christ, we should say "Never !" But when **little temptations** come we slip into them, proving that our hearts are not wholly faithful; and God does look at little things. Here he noted the difference between the larger number and the smaller and He notices private remarks and the way we do things—as in gifts to Him, whether large or small—marking all and testing whether we are fit for Him as He searches into the secret corners of our lives.

Another lesson here out of many is that there is a right and a wrong way of using present circumstances. We are to "use this world as not abusing it," *i.e.* not using it to the full. The 300 took water to quench their momentary thirst ; just enough to satisfy present need. **God** was their first consideration while **self** was of the rest. The world would say the latter are better prepared for fighting. Not so God. There are needs in all our lives—need of rest ; of recreation, etc.—and God knows it and sends them. Jonathan, when faint, took only as much honey as he could get on the end of his staff ; putting God's work before his own refreshment . . . . but where is this seen in the lives of Christians ? Here is a trumpet call from God to lazy, careless lives. God grant it may bear on us and lead us to ask how we each are using present things. Have we partial or entire devotedness to Him ?

9–23. Here are three lines of very striking thoughts with some lessons for us. 1st. The special character of the encouragement given to Gideon as to his confidence in God in the hour of special trial. 2nd. The method and manner of Divine salvation. 3rd. The lesson of the lamps and pitchers, which divides itself into two thoughts. (*a*) The association of grace and nature in God's people. (*b*) An illustration of events to take place at the First Resurrection !

In the encouragement given to Gideon in the miracle of the wet and dry fleece, we see a proof that God's blessing can rest where He chooses. Notice Gideon's difficulties. Out of 10,000, only 300 were chosen to do God's work! This little band and Gideon had to face that host of enemies filling the valley to fight the battle of the Lord! Hence it was obvious that unaided nature must fail before such a foe. But note here God's graciousness to His servant (9–11)! It was as when Christ said to His disciples "Come ye yourselves apart and rest awhile:" and again before leaving them He called them to "Come and dine." A heavenly Master is gracious to His servants. We are apt to forget His true nature and to think He expects too much; but it is our blind unbelief which makes such mistakes. "Judge not the Lord by feeble sense." We here find God taking the initiative in sending Gideon down to the host, knowing his poor spirit needed strengthening; for there is a difference between the heart that does not want to trust and one which is faint and feels its need of stronger faith. God comes to those who trust Him and asks them to trust Him more; and the presence of any fresh difficulties in a path makes these testimonies of God's grace more valued.

11. Gideon was told to go and listen to a dream in the enemy's camp and found God had been before him. He heard something that was not flattering to self (*v.* 13). God was indeed "using the weak things of the world to confound the wise." The Midianites would not think much of "barley-bread" when all the "corn of the land" was in their hands, yet only such was Gideon. It was not even a weapon—not even Gideon's arm—but the power of God behind the means that wrought the overthrow. He did not yet know or understand how God meant to do the work with lamps and pitchers and trumpets, but he was learning the lesson and able to say "When I am weak then am I strong." Where there is "faith as a grain of mustard seed" it can be developed. Where faith is lacking, development is impossible. We may not be far advanced in the path of faith, but God can increase it. We must learn to see the unseen; to feel that which the soul alone can feel. This is not nature but faith. We walk by faith while struggling continually with that

unbelief in the heart which is always with us; holding on to God's promises when we can neither see nor feel.

19–22. See how wonderfully God works! He allowed the men of that host to act naturally in quarrelling one with another—jealous one of another—till every man's sword was against his fellow! Men's hearts working out evil in their own way—suspicion and pride disintegrating their power—until, seeing the sudden light from the torches, they thought themselves betrayed and began to run; for it takes a righteous man to be a bold one. [Though we may see hosts of agnostics and clever sceptics, let us not be afraid of them. They dispute among themselves. The Darwinites of thirty years ago are not the Darwinites now. Midianites rout Amalekites!]

Note secondly, the method and manner of Divine salvation. God was going to work Israel's deliverance *for* His people and yet *with* them; and in quite a different way from the one in which He fought for them when Joshua commanded the sun and moon to stand still until the enemy was killed. Here, God would have a few to work, to shew it was not done without them. But so few, to prove the victory was not by them but by Himself. It is God's ordinary method to work with and by His people. Thus; the sinner's coming to Christ is an independent act. His submission and faith are the submission and trust of his own heart. True, his heart and will have been inclined; but that does not reduce the man to an automaton as some would have it. God calls; and the sinner hears. God invites; and the sinner comes and trusts. A man left to himself might never have come; but the coming and the trusting are yet personal acts. God is the practical sanctifier of His people by the Holy Spirit dwelling in them; leading and helping them to work out God's will; giving them the impulse to will and to work that they may work and follow on and strive after holiness. Yet, unless God "work in them" they cannot "work out their salvation." Truth lies between the two extremes.

16. In this case Israel were not told to take swords but "trumpets, lamps and pitchers!" How natural thought would have ridiculed such implements, as incapable of causing terror to the enemy! Carnal hearts would reason thus;

but it was a man-depreciating and God-glorifying means of working. Thus in 1 Cor. i., the spiritual host of evil is met by spiritual weapons which are " foolishness " in men's sight ; but are really stronger than any of man's selection. How often we are apt to neglect a work because we fancy the *modus operandi* is missing ; as Moses, on the plea of the lack of ready speech. And yet what marvellous miracles he wrought ! So do not despise the little works and little words of every day life. Do the little things God puts before you in His strength, and then you may be sure you are doing His work. Instance the true arguments Naaman's servants used with their master—" If the prophet bade thee do some great thing, wouldest thou not have done it ? How much rather when he says to thee ' Wash and be clean ' ! " Make the little commonplace effort etc., and if you can do nothing else, you can pray. God's means are often such as men would despise—as the earthen pot—but it held the torch, and when broken it revealed the " torch " and worked wonders (*v.* 21) !

Look at the lamps of Gideon's men in the light of 2 Cor. iii.–v. Moses ministered the Law which brought condemnation ; but the Apostles ministered life and righteousness in the Gospel which were wrought out by Christ (*ch. iii.*). Then Paul works this out in a new analogy (*ch. iv.*). This ministry is in earthen vessels ; and he says *I* am not worthy or strong for it, **in order that** the excellency of it may be seen to be not in the vessel but in the Gospel itself. It was not in the material which was earthen, not porcelain ; for the more common the vessel the more obvious is it that the excellency is in the power of God. While working, we are like a pot beginning to crack and the light inside being revealed. So the more we work the more the glory of God becomes visible.

Take the lives of some of God's vessels such as Carey—the cobbler missionary. Men say " what a beautiful character ! " It is not so ; but the grace of God in him was marvellous. He used to say " expect great things of God " as if he knew something of God.

Now let us turn to the illustration of the First Resurrection in this scene of the Lamps and Pitchers. Some say that the Lord will come the second time **secretly.** But no! He will certainly come in the darkest part of the night but **not secretly**; neither does Scripture speak of Christ's people being "caught up" in a moment, though it does say they will be "changed in a moment" **when** the trumpet shall sound like those of Gideon's 300; and then the glorious likeness of Christ, which they will wear after being changed, shall shine out upon the world and be the voucher to the whole universe that Christ's work is done and the bodies of His people redeemed and "conformed to His image!" That moment, when the earthly vessels are broken, shall be the moment of the defeat and dismay of Christ's adversaries. Both will take place at one point of time when the Lord Jesus shall be revealed from Heaven (2 *Thes. i.* 7–10). God's enemies shall flee at the moment the earthly pitchers are broken and then God's glory shall be revealed! "Belovéd; now are we the sons of God; and it doth not yet appear what we shall be: but we know that when he shall appear we shall be like Him, for we shall see Him as He is."

Ch. VIII. God's "Call" to the

1—3 "Men of Ephraim" (Cold-hearted Christians).

5—7 "Men of Succoth" (Mere professors).

8, 9 "Men of Penuel" (Worldlings).

4 "Gideon and his band" (Faint yet pursuing).

All have known periods in their lives in which they realised that some special appeal or "call" was made to their hearts. The converted certainly know of one such "call" to them; and what is true of "conversion-experience" is true of periods when circumstances prove to be a new "call" of God to the soul. It is well if we know how to interpret it and can at once say "Speak Lord," without thinking it a human call as Samuel at first did. Such a call came to David, when, on his father's errand to his brothers he saw Goliath and in God's strength slew him. Also to Levi when doing his accounts, and was called to leave them and follow Christ. Gideon also, though threshing wheat, at once responded, which brought out the events of these chapters. God's calls are a test of the state of the heart. When He appealed to Nabal through David, *he* never thought the request came from God and his answer shewed the selfishness of his heart. God was near and he knew it not, but refused the request and perished. To God's people there often comes a near dealing of God which appeals to them to turn into this or to that path of service for Him, and proves a test as to the state of their hearts. This chapter gives an account of four **bodies** of persons to whom such appeals or " calls " came, and each met it in a different way. **Ephraim** met it by a half response (1–3). **Succoth** by a refusal (4–8). **Penuel** again by a refusal (9) : all of which read us lessons of things which ought **not** to be but which we often find in ourselves. **Gideon** is an example of what we ought to be.

Ephraim was a double tribe—two included in one—and occupying the largest portion of the land, so a very prominent tribe ; but when Gideon was preparing his army to go against the Midianites, it was not to Ephraim he turned but to Zebulon and Naphtali for help (*vi.* 35) ; and out of those small tribes he took only 300 ! Ephraim was not called, for he was utterly unfit for the work and may be taken as an illustration of the **cold-hearted Christian** ; Succoth of the **mere professor** ; Penuel of the **cold blind world** ; but Gideon of **sympathy and yearning over his brethren.** These three **bodies** are around us.

First then, let us contemplate Christians and their work who are swayed by pride, carelessness, selfishness, and so are unfit to do it but who are very difficult to deal with. Ephraim was lacking in earnestness. They had a good country ; were possessed of abundance of flocks and were earnest enough about **them** but not about God or their brethren or the interests of the people of Israel. Wanting too in energy, what they had was given to their own feelings ; and while Gideon was at work, they neither saw nor realised it or they would have gone to him and desired to be joined with him in it. But his work was done before a hand was moved in Ephraim ; and when they did come forward at the moment of victory, it was not in the spirit of service but of conceit and pride, asking why they had not been called ? But they should not have needed to be asked : and in his reply we see how very unworldly Gideon's conduct was.

There are lots of " men of Ephraim " around us in the Church, who by carelessness and false teaching are in the same condition as the Churches to whom St. John wrote in Rev. iii. They do not see that as Christ was rejected so is His Truth ; or, that religion is really a change of heart ; but are anxious to mix up the world with the Church ; to join what God has put asunder. Popular Christianity blinds the inward eye till, like the Laodiceans, men think they see when really they are blind. But Ephraim came right at last ; assisting Gideon in the " work of the Lord " (*vii.* 24), and over them we could write " Better late than never." Faults and failings in Christians must be pointed out by a faithful minister, yet we must be quick to see what good we can find in others. Gideon did not reject their help at the last moment ; so if we seek to follow Christ in a narrower path than others, let us take care it does not blunt our sympathies. Ephraim was far better than the " men of Succoth ; " and if we meet with such as Ephraim who are Christians, let us seek with affection and in a right spirit to lead them in the right way.

Now the " men of Succoth " were in a condition of utter unbelief ; for when Gideon asked them for bread for his men who were faint, their reply inferred that he had not yet fought and might not conquer Zeba and Zalmunna (*v.* 6) ! Hence too their selfishness ! They had no pity for these men nor sympathy with the work they had done. They argued that " if they gave them bread, the enemy might not be defeated and the Midianites still be victors," so they would keep out of it. These then are an illustration of those who, while putting on the name of Christ, are yet of the world. Such shall never enter Heaven, for they were never of it. They take up the Christian position as the Church, but what is their relation to the service of Christ ? Their real attitude is as much one of hostility to it as was that of " the men of Succoth." They have no interest in the purposes of God and care nothing for His Truth or His people. Take *e.g.* those who tortured God's people during the times of the Inquisition and who had no sympathy of heart with the real followers of Christ among men. Remember the lesson of Matt. xxv. at the separation of the sheep and the goats. What is the test as to which are sheep and which goats? This—that the sheep will be found to have cared for what God cared for and to have been interested in those who belonged to Christ. Grace had made them ministers to Christ in His people, while the very opposite was the case with the goats. They had not ministered to Christ through His people. So there are "men of Succoth" to be seen to-day and also "men of Penuel;" men of the world who say the interests of the world are their chief interest. The end of the one was chastisement; of the other destruction (16, 17). Retribution will overtake false professors *and* cold worldlings. God will be justified by and by. The "towers of Penuel" will come down one day and God be glorified in their destruction (*v.* 9).

"Man's day is fast receding, The day of God will come."

Now let us turn to Gideon and his band who were "faint yet pursuing"—one of the loveliest pictures in the Bible. They had served with faithful and unselfish hearts and were now **faint.** Their "spirit was willing, but the flesh weak." They had no food; were weary; yet going on! Cannot you see the difference? Carelessness there. Carefulness here. Selfishness and pride *versus* pursuing to the end. And not only a contrast between God's serving people and the world, but between God's people who are serving Him and God's people who are not! Some of us know what it is to be faint in spiritual things. "Serving the Lord" is sure to bring troubles. It often leads to the cave of Adullam; but that is the right place. So don't give up but "keep the Word of God's endurance." Let us be sure we follow the right path and that God calls us to it, and though "ready to faint yet pursue." From Gideon we learn one lesson out of many; *viz.* the beautiful union of firmness and gentleness in dealing with Ephraim in his answer to their murmurings. His wisdom is seen in **not** saying many things he might have said. He minimised his own services to them (*v.* 2). How wise and yet how gentle! Some of us are very decided but not very gentle. Others are gentle but lack decision. A combination of both is needed. God grant that our attitude to His work be like that of this wise good Gideon.

22–35. Over this passage may be written "Prosperity and Decay" both with reference to Gideon and the Nation. It contains a lesson to corporate bodies and to individuals. . . . Our dangers are both external and internal. The tendency of modern teaching is to direct attention to inward evil as formerly it was to outward evil. Satan is active and we have to wrestle against wicked spirits. But suppose there were no devil or that he were bound as he will be in the next dispensation, there would still be conflict as there will be in Millennium; for in every one there is an evil heart of unbelief in departing from the living God—a spring of evil welling up in us—upon which Satan works. So, surrounding circumstances are not wholly to blame for our failures as we are liable to think. Satan is ever ready to take advantage of circumstances to tempt our hearts; but there is the proneness to sin within. Just because we are what we are, days of prosperity have their peculiar temptation as well as days of adversity. Temptations come to us all in our lives. We need to learn from Scripture their **character**: so that if we are seeking to be guided by God we may be delivered from them.

First then, we have Gideon's individual history; and secondly, Israel's corporate history. Consider the dangers to which **we** are prone in prosperity and notice those into which Gideon did not fall; then those into which he did. We are exhorted in Eph. vi. to be clothed with armour, so that we may stand against the **wiles** (not the might) of an enemy who, if he cannot come in one form to beguile, will come in another. In a day of prosperity the great danger is pride, *e.g.* Uzziah; Nebuchadnezzar; etc.; but Gideon did not fall a prey to that. His heart was not lifted up. There was humility in his reply (*v.* 22–23). Another danger of prosperity is sloth, from the unbending of the bow—a tendency to sleep instead of watching—and *that* did not entangle Gideon's feet, for his efforts continued; but it may ours. Another danger is Selfishness: making self the beginning and end of our religion. This also Gideon did not fall into (*see v.* 35), a beautiful conclusion.

There is no perfect character in Scripture and on this good man came one sad blight. His failure came in the matter of the Ephod (*v.* 27) which is not easy to understand. Having been asked to be ruler of Israel, should he or should he not have refused? Noting his humility, we say if by being Judge he should displace God's kingly relation to Israel, he was certainly right to refuse. But we must remember that all the deliverers raised up by God did judge Israel and that Gideon himself virtually did; so that it would not have been wrong to take up the reins of authority. He was right to refuse for his son and his son's son who had not been called of God. Moses judged them, so did Samuel and at that point began Gideon's failure. It is as easy to fail in not acting as in acting; for had Gideon accepted the office, Israel were ready to follow him, and he was doing it, though without feeling the responsibility. Had he felt the responsibility of his position, he might never have made and set up that Ephod. He was in a public relation to Israel and led them; thus he made two mistakes which were two sins. First in refusing to take the position to which God called him—which **call** was very much more clear than that of many of the other judges; Shamgar *e.g.*—but the responsibility of the call extended further than the subduing of the people of the east; so he took a wrong position. He would **not** be the civil governor, but he **would** be a priest (24–27)! What gave him this inclination? There must have been some current in his soul drawing him to this, for he might have put another in office. He may have had a desire to constitute himself the channel of communication between God and the people as Saul, who forced himself into the position of "priest" with the result that he was rejected by God as "king (1 *Sam. xiii*)!" Again we have Uzziah; a good "king," but he sought to be "priest" as well; which spoilt all his life (2 *Ch. xxvi.* 16–21)!

It was this same sin Gideon committed. The Ephod was the special garment of the High Priest and the one which bare the Urim and Thummim, by means of which God com municated with Israel. This one of Gideon may have been associated with spiritualism, into which perhaps he had been drawn. Moreover, Ophrah was the place chosen by God in which to put His Name. Gideon's sin was as mysterious as it was bad . . . as men who are at one time agnostic; at another rationalistic! Gideon evidently regarded it in the light of a sacramental ordinance; seeing the visible thing and imagining the reality was behind it! And this evil spread till all Israel went after it instead of to Shiloh, where the Ark of God was (*v.* 27)!

There is a striking lesson to be learnt from ver. 23. Gideon ought to have accepted the position of being Israel's earthly ruler by the "call of God," and he did take it, but failed because not realising his responsibility. We find a parallel to this in the principle established by God in the Church as seen in Eph. iv. 11. "He gave some Apostles and some prophets and some pastors and teachers," showing, that though God did not give apostles and prophets in a **permanent** relation, He did give pastors and teachers **for all time.** This blessèd truth has been exaggerated into a curse, by "pastors" being made into priests and "teachers" into rulers and masters until they are turned into "popes;" and we know with what evil results. On the other hand, there is now a revolt from this error into one in the opposite direction. The truth of "pastorship" is reduced to a nullity, so that government in the Church is either an oligarchy or a tyranny. This was Gideon's error. He was "king" all the time, yet not the acknowledged Head of Israel. . . . Had he acted as Judge, he might have been a great blessing in upholding GOD's kingship. So with the Church. Christ should be the chief Shepherd and Pastor; the pastors His under-shepherds, recognising their responsibility. If such dare to decline the pastorship for which they are fitted, they may lead away from God (*v.* 27)! But if they rule and lead according to God, they are to be had in remembrance and valued (*Heb. xiii.* 7). [The idea among Brethren is, that none should take that post; but, if God give "pastors" let us acknowledge them and let them seek to carry out the office, recognising the responsibility of it. What a blessing Gideon might have been to Israel had he guided them away from Ophrah sins]!

Ch. IX. Abimelech. Jotham's parable. This chapter contains the story of events which occurred after Gideon's death. He left seventy sons besides one by a Canaanitish woman. The last years of his life were the saddest. The establishment of the Ephod seems to have led to a laxity of morals, and his son by this woman slew his brethren and by fraud pushed himself into a prominent place (*v.* 1–6) ! There is not a single ray of light amid the darkness of this chapter. There are three thoughts in it. I. The world laid open to us here is a picture of that in which we live, where sin reigns. II. How *we* should live in this world and discharge our duties in it (*v.* 9–13). Let us be just what God has made us, whether vines, olives, or figs ; but not brambles. III. The providential government of God in the world.

Now take that Shechem world and see how our circumstances are illustrated by this chapter. It is a place in which are two elements that are making up human society now ; *viz.*, those who do not worship God but Baal and those who, however failing, do know and worship God. Forgetfulness of God marked the Shechemites. "God was not in all their thoughts." All their plans, concerns, etc. were executed apart from Him. "God is naught" was in their thoughts if not on their lips. All plans were formed without reference to Him. Independence of God was their principle ! Then they fell into Idolatry—for man was formed to be dependent—and manufactured a god on which to lean (*v.* 4, 46) ! The Shechemites were probably half Canaanites and some the children of mixed marriages ; a debasing element. We see also there what may be seen elsewhere ; *viz.*, the influence of "lust" over anyone ; not only grosser lust, but the serving the desires of one's own heart so as to make all else subservient, as Abimelech did to his lust of power. This reigned there as in our own times. Men argue that Society is become more moral, and yet anyone can note that the controlling motive in the present day is "**pleasure**" whether among high or low ; in Grosvenor Square or Bethnal Green.

Take one example. We find Sunday now looked on as "man's day" not God's ; and man takes it to use for his own purposes! We cannot make people religious by law, but, when Christianity was purer, insensibly God's people had more influence, and they did not go out to enjoy golf, music, etc. as now, when men use God's day for themselves. Dinner parties on Sunday are common now! This disuse and misuse of God's day shew that we live in a world "lust" rules; *i.e.*, where what a man wants to do is the rule and where there is hatred of God's restrictions; forgetting that we are here to do God's will. Remember we live in a Shechem world. Worldliness is around us like the atmosphere. A chink in the armour of our souls and it rushes in; but God puts in us a holy resisting power, that we may be in it but not of it.

7–15. We have here the first parable on record. When Gideon's sons were slain, one was left who, hiding himself, escaped; and while the Shechemites were rejoicing over their king, they heard a voice addressing them in protest. Standing on Mount Gerizim, Jotham was near enough to be heard. This is a striking example of how God's people should be prepared to testify to the world for Him. Abimelech was king—a man whose hands were imbrued in the blood of his seventy brethren—when suddenly sounded a voice of protest! Jotham's were wise words but grievously unheeded, though fulfilled; viz. that while they were rejoicing and forgetting God, their bramble king would in the end be as a fire to destroy them. This prediction was fulfilled to the letter.

The parable teaches us that God has given us our place in the world, and when we discern it, let us understand that just as God makes a vine a vine, an olive an olive, a fig-tree a fig-tree, so He makes His people what they are and expects them to be that and nothing else. Here, Abimelech said "I'll exalt myself" as if God were not, though He has said "He that exalteth himself shall be abased;" and Abimelech came to a shameful death by a woman (*v.* 53)! God brought him down to a place of shame; but if we keep the place God puts us in, He will honour it and we are bound to take it. If God put a man up he must be prepared to fill that higher place. A bramble must not seek to be an olive or a vine or a fig-tree. There is such a thing as going forward *or* backward unholily. It is a comfort to know that to be right is to be in God's hand to be led and guided; trusting to His judgment and call; not shrinking back if He call, but not going forward unless He call. God can only guide in His way the meek and those depending on Him.

9. The olive-tree says " Why should I leave my fatness ? " *i.e.* oil, by which God is honoured and which is useful to men. So we as believers should realise God intends we should be useful and be really vines or olives or fig-trees; but never brambles. We owe a debt to the world around to be as sign-posts pointing to heaven. Just as the olive-tree should not leave its oil to be wasted, so must we not wrap ourselves up in our own selfishness, for God made us for the use of others.

10, 11. The " fig-tree " is used in a different way. It has sweetness and fruit, shewing that God intends His people to have a combination of these, though at the same time the world will hate them as it hated Christ. Fruit may be sour; and alas ! sincere Christians often lack sweetness. True Christians are often not nice persons. The image of Christ is the most beautiful imaginable and it is to that, that God will at the Day of Christ's return conform us !

13. Then the " vine." Its wine was useful in the sacrifices and useful for men. Should all this be given up to be king ? God formed His people that they should make others happy in the highest sense, and in the Millennium they will be a wondrous means of happiness to man. Now, they are often obliged for the moment to make them unhappy in order to bring them to true happiness, as Paul with the jailer at Philippi. Though the world hate us, our ministry to it is really to make it happy; and if there were more of the joy of heaven in our souls, how many more we should make happy and joyful ! and is there any joy like bringing true happiness to another ? Then God warns us by Abimelech not to be brambles—*i.e.* worthless; no good to any—though the elements of the bramble are in our hearts, and men apart from God are worthless (*Rom. vi.* 21). The " bramble " is also unattractive; repulsive; and has no fruit. The hard spiney bramble of the desert is a thornbush to be given a wide berth. In Hell everyone will hate everyone else.

Worldly men try to get on together, but they admit of each other that at the best they are unattractive. The repulsiveness is there though often veiled.

15. As here, the bramble will be the means of conflagration. It is awful to think men can so live as to sink others into perdition! Bramble-bush lives should be avoided; so seek from God to see and know what you are. Live not so that when you die your life will be blotted out, but live to be a happy influence and there will be something in you for which men shall praise God.

Ch. X. Some parts of Scripture are best fitted for "instruction," while others are more adapted for "exhortation" or for **pressing back** on the soul the force of the lessons already learnt but which have only imperfectly taken hold of our hearts. God teaches by "line upon line," so the same truths come again and again to re-impress and to influence the heart more and more. This little chapter is an instance. There is nothing needing much exposition in it. At the same time, it speaks of deep, holy, profitable experience and may act as a reminder of what has been only imperfectly learnt. It is a word of "exhortation" so do not reject it as having heard it before. It may be called a page from the school-book of God from which to learn lessons of His dealings. [There is such a thing as an unholy interest in holy things. Such an interest is unsanctified and becomes a snare to the soul.] We see in it the lessons, the Teacher and His heart; the subject being divided into five parts. i. The apathy into which Israel fell. ii. Their declension and falling away. iii. Their chastisement (God punishing them for His own glory). iv. Their repentance. v. God's restoring mercy.

1. "After Abimelech" (not that he was one of the Judges for he was not called by God; his course being one of self-exaltation), "there arose to defend Israel" *i.e.* to deliver—for the Hebrew word is connected with the name Judges—which should be **saviours**; all of whom were saviours from the enemy before they became Judges. Gideon especially, though when afterwards called to "judge" Israel he failed. Of Tola little is written. He rose when there

was no enemy or evil occurrent. We are not told if he **delivered** Israel but he " **judged** twenty-three years; died and was buried." This episode coming after the troublous times impresses us with the peaceful state of the land; and when Jair arose (*v.* 3) little more is said; yet one significant thing is mentioned *viz.*, that " his thirty sons rode on thirty asses (*v.* 4)!" Now the ass was the animal of state and of luxury, as the horse is with us; so these thirty sons were young aristocrats and put in the place of nobility; in leading places; with material profit to themselves—for thirty cities were allotted to them in Gilead—the most fertile part of the Land! This fact suggests the character of the times. Evidently there had been a change to those of luxury and worldly-mindedness from the former ones of trouble, etc.; and instead of guiding Israel rightly, Jair had used those prosperous times to exalt himself and his family like the great and good Samuel, who gave **his** sons places of honour and authority! Thus he is not mentioned with honour.

Times of relief are apt to become times of Apostasy. When trouble is removed, there comes a great danger of neglect of the soul; a congealing into selfishness; and such conditions are those of extreme danger. " The hand of the diligent shall bear rule" is a proverb of wide application. When the soul is diligently giving effect to every word of Truth that comes to it, that one becomes a means of great helpfulness to others; whereas slothfulness in regard to what God gives of Truth leads a man to become servant of that which he should rule and to get by his own fault into difficulties; his difficulties being his master. Such an one feels held down and can do nothing but cast himself upon God for help. Apathy is followed by selfishness, sloth, pride; so that men become the servants of sins! Some seem to live too long—their grace seemingly worn out—instead of their " path being as a shining light." So this apathy in Israel led to evil. Notice the list of false gods they served (*v.* 6)! There was a complete encompassing; a circle of idolatry around them like the world **we** have to deal with. Can you tell me any place where you can shut out the world? Certainly not in a nunnery; for you take it in with you in your own heart. God allows it to press on us that we may resist it. "Ye have not yet resisted unto blood striving against sin" is a verse full of nerve and force. Are we conscious of evil around? That is not enough. Our call is to resist it; to stand against it. Much of the "holiness teaching" is the reverse of this; as if Scripture did not say we are to strive against sin. We must not only trust but strive also. God will conquer our enemies *in* us and *through* us.

6. Now notice how this declension of Israel is divided. They served Baalim etc., and then forsook the Lord! Their first sin was compromise. They served God, but felt they must respect other people's opinions and not be uncharitable. But Israel were commanded **not** to get on with their neighbours; yet this was what they sought to do—compromise—thinking probably to teach the heathen the way of the Lord, though consenting to go to *their* feasts; till gradually *they* served the heathen gods and forsook the Lord! Declension which begins with compromise goes on to forsaking God; to subordinating the principles of God to the maxims of the world until God's are forgotten. In the physical world there are poisons all round us, but a healthy body has power to resist their hostile influence; so the soul must have a resisting power wherewith to meet moral poisons around, and here it is that God's grace comes in. If we do not compromise His Truth, He will give Grace as a resisting power in our souls that will keep them from the evil.

7. Here is the next lesson. A point very imperfectly realised by us all is, that God is angry with His children sometimes; thus we confuse the **judicial** wrath of God with His wrath as a **Father.** Others again say that the anger in both cases is the same. But His **judicial** wrath against sin is quenched once for all when the sinner is brought under the shelter of the Blood of the Lamb by faith. God's gifts are unrepented of. When He gives peace and pardon He never takes it back. A sinner once brought into the family of God is never put out again, and such an one can say "There is no condemnation to them that are in Christ Jesus." But God, as a **Father,** can be angry with His children without putting them out of His family; or as a **Master** if they do not serve Him. His anger was hot against His servant

Jehoshaphat (2 *Ch. xix.*) ! It is important to understand this. It is His children He chastises. His anger was hot against Israel because they were His people, and believers need to pray for pardon as the Lord taught his disciples. The sins of believers are referred to in 1 John ii. 1.

10. Note the repentance of Israel in which there were three steps. First, the feeling of need of repentance ; and when this change of mind takes place, results must follow as in 2 Cor. vii. 10, 11. It was but the dawn of light here, for they had not realised the evil of their sin and ingratitude. " Did I not, etc. (*v.v.* 11–13)? " " Yet ye have forsaken Me ! " God had done more for them than they thought of ; and we, like them, have taken God's daily blessings as a matter of course.

14. It is good to be permitted to come to the lowest point. It was doubtless or probably a prophet who gave them this message to go to their own agencies for help, and *then* like many others who have long prayed prayerless prayers, Israel began really to pray when they found those on whom they had leaned fail.

15. The third step in their repentance was a holy contrition full of great faith. " Do Thou with us whatsoever seemeth good unto Thee." One would not want to fall into hands that could not be trusted. The more we come to the end of self the nearer we get to God. May God grant us personal dealings of this kind.

16. God's restoring mercy. We could not understand God unless He compared Himself to a man—a proof Scripture comes from Him. He cannot repent but He can feel and love and grieve and pity over His suffering people ; and these words teach us measurably about Him. The truly forgiven soul feels the sweetness of pardon and the horror of the sin that is pardoned. The words of Ps. cxxx. are those of a pardoned instructed saint. How many deliverers God *can* bring to the help of His people ! We need to realise our need of that help.

Ch. XI. History of Jephthah. This book contains undulating experiences of God's people. The story changes from dark to light and from light to dark ; and the dark is often very dark while some characters are often very blessed. Among those who are " of faith " there are great differences of level as to developments. Thus Gideon was not on so high a level of spiritual development as Deborah. Jephthah was still lower ; and what can we say of Samson ? Yet there was something in all worthy of being spoken of in Heb. xi. which Jephthah was. He was a Gileadite. Former judges had been connected with the northern part of the land, but the history now passes to the east near Moab. It is strange that the southern tribe of Judah is scarcely mentioned as yet. Why, we cannot say. Jephthah's life began in the dark shade of disgrace and sorrow, his mother probably being a Syrian idolater and he thrust out by the rest of his family as being half-Gentile, which was a cause of reproach. His mother doubtless came from Tob whither he fled, and he seems to have been anything but a holy character, for vain fellows gathered to him ; seeking affinity and leading a predatory raiding life with him. Such was Jephthah ! Yet even in him is seen a touch of the grace of God, which had taught him that Israel's God is the true God and that it was the truest honour to serve Him and work under the direction of His providence.

[1–3. These verses are an interlude ; and ver. 4 returns to or follows ch. x. 18 : shewing there was no one to withstand the children of Ammon making war upon Israel in Gilead, which had to bear the brunt of it.]

5–9. He evidently had a reputation for boldness and skill ; and yet there must have been some softness in his character making him anxious to be linked with Israel. His using the word " home " shewed his heart was there. Hitherto he had been independent of them but not against them ; still there was much of nature in his desire to be " head " (*v.* 9). He would be that or nothing ! There may also have been wisdom in his desire, for no one else seemed so fitted to lead in that rough time. We can't judge of him according to present modes of society or according to what St. Paul was ; but must remember the low state of morals at that period.

11. Jephthah " uttered all his words before the Lord," shewing he was a believer and fully realised that he took this position under a sense of responsibility to God ; believing

that **He** had arranged for him to have the headship and wished others to be impressed with his appointment to deliver Israel from God's enemies. This is the brightest part of Jephthah's history.

12–23. Then we come to the terms of the negotiations between the Ammonites and Jephthah. He thoroughly identifies himself with Israel and throws off all association with Gentiles. The answer of the king of Ammon was spurious and untrue; but Jephthah's shewed acquaintance with Israel's past history as related in Numbers. It was the land of the **Amorites** God gave them (v. 15, 21).

24. Here is seen the character of Jephthah's mind; his light and his darkness. It is impossible to touch pitch and not be defiled. God said Israel's separation was to be definite and total. Jephthah's idea was, that the god of each nation was good in its own way and that Israel's God was as one of them, though perhaps the greatest. He had not realised that God is God alone and an idol nothing: so he spoke thus to the enemy!

27–29. Here he solemnly invokes God to judge between them; nevertheless the Ammonites came to war against him! The Spirit of the Lord coming upon him would not alone prove that he was a partaker of saving grace, for some who had not, possessed "gifts of the Spirit" as Balaam and Saul; though afterwards deprived of them. It was this that caused David to pray that governmental gifts should not be taken from him as from Saul (Ps. li. 11); and God gave Jephthah His Spirit to fit him for this work; which may also be said of Samson.

30, 31. But he first did a strange act, though we must remember the strange circumstances of emergency in which he was. Here was this mass of alien foes coming on Gilead towards the comparative handful of Israelites, and he did what was generally done by heathen generals. Feeling unable alone to cope with the difficulties of the situation, he makes this strange vow to the Lord. Though the neuter gender is used, Jephthah could have had no idea of offering an inanimate object or any unclean animal; so it must have referred to a person (what else could have come out of a house?) that he promised to offer! We must judge of him just where he was and by the tone of things around him, though the idea is abhorrent to our minds. He started, believing God would help him, which He did ; for he subdued the enemy and smote twenty cities !

34-37. He never expected that this daughter—his only child—would meet him. He probably had a large household and doubtless imagined some slave dependent on him would come out to receive him on his return ; but in the providence of God his daughter did ! What a natural scene between them (*v.* 35-39) ! " And he did with her according to his vow," so he must have offered her up in sacrifice. Some, thinking to soften this scene of horror, say she was not sacrificed but led the life of a recluse, aiming at giving warrant to the principle of social suicide by becoming nuns, which Scripture nowhere countenances. They say Jephthah deprived her of social life as with Romish priests and nuns ; but we must regard this principle as wrong and evil. This bewailing her virginity upon the mountains with her friends cannot mean she became a nun, for we find the bright spot in the chapter in her dutiful submission to her father's vow ; not seeing it would have been more honourable to break it than to keep it. She bewailed that, for her, all hope was over of helping to build up the nation of Israel as Hannah. There is no question but that this girl willingly submitted to be sacrificed ! [This scene has moral and spiritual lessons for us. Is it right to make vows ? Though we must not judge Jephthah by our manner of life, one who makes a vow virtually undertakes to act in independence of God ; to decide by his own wisdom what should be done instead of saying " If the Lord will, I will do this and that." So, have nothing to do with vows and covenants. *e.g.* Israel's vow at Sinai. How quickly it was broken ! Remember too Jacob's evil vow, and how unnecessary after God's promise to him of undeserved blessing !]

Notice again ; God forbade all mingling with heathen nations ; one of their chief principles being, to offer their children in the fire (*see* 2 *Kings iii.* 26 *and Micah vi.* 7), which even Manasseh did ! But God saw in it the false idea, that in order to please Him something must be given to Him ; but even **that** would be as nothing ! He requires us to know and to love Him, and such a gift as this would offend Him (*Acts xvii.* 25). Jephthah's mind, in the emergency in which he found himself, was swayed by superstition as Rahab's when she told the lie, though she hid the spies in faith. The moment we think to act independently of God, we begin to do wrong. If we know God's character, let us act on it and remember that He does not need to be made our Debtor.

Ch. XII. The Evil of Pride. Read 1 Cor. xiii. in contrast to the spirit exhibited here. In the Book of Judges we come to pages dark and solemn; finding records of terrible blots of failures in those who were really people of God. This is seen in the chastisements He inflicted on them; and there are many instructive lessons to be learnt from the various ways in which they rejected Him. The strife here arose from the common passion of wounded pride, lest others should occupy the position which it was feared they had lost. They were a double tribe—Ephraim and Manasseh—inheriting Joseph's blessing in Gen. xlix. 22–26 and we sometimes find the blessing of the whole nation centred in this one (*Ps. lxxviii.* 1). Ephraim was celebrated for warlike prowess; was a prominent tribe and one God had greatly blessed; but blessing had stimulated their pride. Though Joshua allotted them an ample inheritance they were discontented, and that temper of mind underlies the whole of the transaction recorded here.

The first lesson is this. How pride works for the dishonour of God in the hearts even of God's people, leading to actions dictated by the fleshly mind and the impulse of Satan! Ver. 2 proves the accusation in v. 1 to be untrue. There are those who like nothing to be done unless suggested by themselves though they would not act at the instigation of another; and here wounded pride galled them. Pride is the very essence of all sin, and is allied with kindred ones: as *e.g.* pride and sloth; pride and lying; pride and cruelty. There was no desire here for God's glory, but when the work was done they were ready to rise in defence of their own glory, yet they had been guilty of "not coming to the help of the Lord against the mighty!" The human heart is ever the same, and what took place in their hearts may also take place in ours. Pride may be called the seed-sin; the root-sin; out of which a whole tree of evil may spring. You may say you have a right to stand up for yourself and vindicate your own rights; but in so doing how many evils may follow! Oh! the cruel things Christians do when pride takes possession of the heart! We have only to recall the cruelties perpetrated in forcing episcopacy on the Scottish Covenanters. It is always the same in every religious persecution; and these principles may exist in our own hearts. When we are standing up for self, our face is turned away from God and we are acting in opposition to Him. Pride wishes to take God's place, but He "resisteth the proud." Look at the mischief wrought in this case—42,000 being slain! In our case it may not be lives that are taken, but what havoc the records of eternity may disclose as the result of this deadly evil! Oh! be humble, for you don't know what misery you may entail upon yourself and others.

5, 6. Gilead's cruelty. See here how another passion flamed and blazed. This slaughter of 42,000 was perfectly needless and cruel. Here we have the history of the evil in the human heart unless the grace of God dwell in it! Although there may never have been an action in our lives to be compared to this, we know not what *might* be **wrought out in our lives** if pride and cruelty be reigning in our hearts. I have seen it. There is no limit to the evil unless God restrain; for there is such evil within, that if God allowed the veil to be taken off it would shock us! What evil will not the annals of Christendom reveal? and they might repeat themselves in our hearts but for the restraining grace of God!

6. Two great spiritual lessons flow from this simple verse. First, that small things are a test of character. What a very little thing this was! Some clever Gileadite or possibly Jephthah himself (for he was a clever man) thought of this test. The language of the tribes on the eastern side of Jordan had become mingled with that of their Syrian neighbours while Ephraim retained the purer Hebrew pronunciation, so that it presented an inference that could not be avoided. Without time to consider, out came the word "Sibboleth" and out flashed the sword and the man lay dead at his feet! So it is the small things of life that are the most unerring

tests of character. Small actions; little words show more what a man is than the greater and more important transactions in life. This fact has given rise to many popular proverbs, *e.g.* "No man is a hero to his own valet." He may be a lion in the field, but the every day details of his life shew what the man is. Nothing suits in the hour of danger but the mother tongue. It is a deeply humbling lesson to remember this. Remember it for yourselves, your wives; your children; your servants; your fellow Christians; the world at large. There are many "Sibboleths" in life which shew wise men what we are. They should lead us to seek God's help and to take care when the test comes to say "Shibboleth;" proving that we are what we have seemed to be. God's grace is sufficient for this. We might carefully draw out a code of 10,000 rules, yet a "Sibboleth" at the end would trip us up if seeking our own honour. Regeneration and sanctification are needed if the "Sibboleth" of the evil heart is to be kept down.

Another lesson. In religious questions judge by great guiding truths not by details. Both Shibboleth and Sibboleth meant the same thing—a stream. On this simple fact observe the lesson, that distinction needs to be drawn between persons who are right in intention and those who are otherwise. It can never be love to pass over what is wrong or to mingle right and wrong and call it Christian love. Yet we continually meet with those who mean right—true children of God—but with whom there is an obliquity in the way they carry out what they seek to do and we must not confuse one who means right with one who means wrong. If a thing be wrong nothing can justify it. Wrong doctrine is not the same as Truth. There is an everlasting distinction between them. Separation from evil is a duty but the danger is, lest the spirit of separation should get the highest place in the heart and slay the brother. Tolerance again must be joined with firmness.

We learn four brief lessons from Jephthah's life. I. He is an example of one in whom faith and superstition mingled. Take care that your light be not dimmed by darkness. Protestantism has lost much of its influence because adulterated with Romanism.

II. We see in Jephthah boldness and decision; enabling him to take a right course at a right time. How often when the time for decision comes we are not bold: but Jephthah's words were duly ratified by his deeds. Never **say** more than it is right to **do**; but when you have said what is right, be bold to do it.

III. There was a grievous absence of right wisdom here such as Gideon displayed towards the Ephraimites. **He** spoke words that quieted their wrath, displaying both meekness and wisdom (*ch. viii.* 2)! Not so Jephthah. It is a great thing to keep the tongue behind the teeth until the truth makes it necessary to speak. "The words of the wise are spoken in quiet." There is nothing more evil than the way we sometimes talk; and "the beginning of strife is as when one letteth out water."

IV. With all his faults Jephthah judged Israel (*v.* 7). His life was a solitary lonely one. He had no home joys. He left no child and probably never married again; and what wonder, with the remembrance of that awful mistake and sin which was renewed every year when the daughters of Jerusalem went annually to commemorate the sad tragedy! His life bore the scar of that sin but it kept him from falling into the like again. He set himself to do the work appointed him and he did it, which was strangely different from the one before, who had thirty sons riding on thirty ass colts! These are solemn lessons we have had before us and should make us ashamed and also afraid of ourselves. May they drive us closer to that blessèd One who is our All in All. Our pardon for the past. Our holiness for the present and our heaven of eternal blessedness for the future!

Ch. XIII. The history of the Judges consists of prominent individuals raised up by God and of lessons from their lives. To-day we come to the last, but not the least instructive one—Samson. His history is one of direction but also more of correction; and it is painful that so much should have been for correction; but it is a wholesome fact and should lead us to self-examination.

1. An important principle is enunciated and illustrated by these circumstances of destroying punishments. We

find two things moving together, *viz.* Divine sovereignty and human responsibility. God acting, and yet His act determined by human action and sin! Israel did evil and the Lord delivered them into the hands of the Philistines forty years. The parallelism is seen in God being the Arbiter of all events yet man's action determining experience. We see now in riddles; and if we refuse to submit to riddles which we cannot understand we shall be as if shut in a cage. God places us within the limits of certain truths and we may learn a little; but we must act within the limits of our common knowledge. Where there is Truth let us recognise Truth, and if we cannot piece all we must leave it till all is made plain. Man is a responsible being. If he sin, he sins of his own will but he is not to say "I must sin" or it will bring on him corresponding consequences. So here; Israel chose to sin in allying themselves with the idolatrous families around and then the Lord delivered them into the hand of the Philistines in judgment! God's action was a correction to the sin which brought it down. Human action is not automatous; but man is responsible to God. God help us to accept this truth and regard it as a solemn fact before us in every-day life.

The story of this chapter brings us round the country to the coast. Israel had truckled with Sidonians, Syrians, Ammonites, Amalekites, Moabites, etc.; and had gone the round of evil. As God delivered them from one they went on to the next, and now they had come to the Philistines on the coast of the south. This gives a solemn picture of the human heart. If there are five doors for evil to enter it, it will enter by all! But for God's restraints, where might any of us be this instant? The possibilities of our evil nature are infinite!

1. A brief chronicle with no comment.

2. Another fact chronicled is of a childless man of the tribe of Dan (the worst tribe), into which God entered in grace! All that Jacob could say of Dan when blessing his sons was (after describing him as a serpent and an adder), "I have waited for Thy salvation, O Lord!" meaning he was still waiting for a blessing for Dan! Yet to this evil tribe and a childless home an action of grace came unsought and

unasked with the message (*v.* 7); an illustration of another lesson, *viz.* that man's blessing and deliverance and help always come from God and they come into circumstances of human evil unasked. What is Grace? Our hearts need to be taught that Grace is favour unbought; undeserved; dependable on the mind of Him who bestows it without being asked. God is the God of all grace, and Grace is never seen to be Grace except in such circumstances as this of badness and barrenness. Israel's deliverance here does not seem to have been determined by their cry as elsewhere. The story begins with God's action. Think once more of the meaning of the word "Grace;" not as a theological word but as a famished soul looks on bread and water; as a captive hears the key turn in the lock of his dungeon; as the sick man begins to realise the hope of cure. But for Grace, anyone of us would have perished eternally; and it comes to us because the Father's heart is toward the lost one. Samson's history is a history of God's Grace. Think of the misery and helplessness in Israel when God entered the scene with this promise and He had Grace enough for these days as for Samson's. Shall we then continue in sin that Grace may abound? No! Grace **shall** abound but not in the midst of evil continued in.

Note an important fact here. In what aspect should we view Samson's life? Some speak of him as a type of Christ, causing infidels to sneer. Many mistakes are made as to "types." Nearly all errors in doctrine are founded on what *men* call "types," so that a sober interpretation is discredited and God's Word is not had in reverence. We must never force our own interpretation of Scripture. Many would be the incongruities of taking Samson as a type of Christ. Scripture nowhere says he was, and **we** must not say so of anyone, unless assured of it by Scripture, though we may use such as illustrations and learn many lessons, *e.g.* Samson with the gates of Gaza illustrates Christ's victory over death. Scripture says the "veil of the Temple was a **type** of the flesh of Christ." Melchizedec and Aaron were; and Adam too is said to be "a **type** (not a figure) of One to come." To say *e.g.* "**we** can see one to be a **type**" will lead to error. (A writer of a "Book on Types" has become a

" universalist " and has since written " The mysteries of the kingdom of heaven." Types are not mysteries, but are to unfold mysteries ; so call nothing a **type** except as Scripture warrants it). Samson is not a **type** of Christ, though parts of his history illustrate His work ; and the best part of his history is the being mentioned in Heb. xi. **All** those results of Faith were not realised in any **one** individual mentioned there, so seek for which result can be identified with either of those mentioned in vv. 32–37. Samson may be with two only—" out of weakness made strong ; " and " turned to flight the armies of aliens." Though we may not imagine so, it is inferred that he was a weak small man or why should the Philistines ask where his great strength was ? He had a supernatural strength given him by God : it was not mere muscle.

Paul seems to be the New Testament Samson. In 2 Cor. xii. he says " God's strength is made perfect in his weakness." That was his experience ; and again " When I am weak then am I strong." Samson never learnt that lesson. He always thought he had strength and could use it apart from God ! His hair was only a symbol of his strength, and he was weak as water as soon as God withdrew His supernatural power. Note also his Nazarite birth. It was miraculous as in other cases of God's working for blessing (*e.g.* Isaac's), for God would have Israel down the ages to know that blessing came in miraculous birth. Thus also Samuel and John Baptist, whom God sent in the times of Israel's darkest history. And greatest of all miraculous births was His through Whom God interposed in Grace ; and Samson was to be a Nazarite that God might make plain the principle on which He would deal with men. Four things are required of a Nazarite. Obedience to God. Separation from evil. Self-control ; and a realization that all strength of life comes from God. Samson took this path but failed in it by leaving God. Are *we* seeking to walk in that separate path ? If our lives are not separate lives they are useless ; but God will give strength for it. This history teaches what we may be and what we are not to be. The object of the Book of Judges is to teach lessons of spiritual experience as to the secret of strength amid weakness and failure, and we are taught by the characters brought before us in it. The history of the prominent one now before us is given in great detail, not because it is a record of the best character or in praise of Samson, but because we need so much teaching as to how and why *we* go wrong. These details are given for our learning and are intended to point the contrast between divine power and wisdom **and** human weakness and folly in those who ought to have known better.

Notice him first as an example of folly and weakness; and secondly as an example of wisdom and strength bestowed upon the servants of God. Note his origin. He was of the tribe of Dan. (Zorah was probably partly in Dan and partly in Judah). It is a sorrowful history of this tribe in Gen. xlix. 16–18. Contrast the "blessings," pronounced on all the other tribes. Though Jacob had waited, he did not see one for Dan! It became a divided tribe and was the source of idolatry which went on to the time of the captivity! Jeroboam set up one of his calves in Dan and in Chronicles and Rev. vii. Dan is omitted! The only bright spot is in Ezek. xlviii. 1 where the tribe is allowed a position, though in the extreme north; the furthest point from the Tabernacle of Jehovah.

In one sense every servant of God comes from the tribe of Dan. It shews that the grace that saves from the lowest point of human history avails for the worst of sinners. There is a touching word in v. 5.—" he shall **begin** to save Israel." It is one of the saddest things in Samson's history that he was always beginning but what he began was not finished. He did not effectually deliver Israel from the Philistines. The most that can be said of him is, that he **began.** See the folly and weakness of human nature at its best. It is always bad; but note the character of Divine wisdom and strength in contrast, in his miraculous birth. In all such cases there was a work to be done; and it was always accomplished by the strength of God. It was not generation so to speak, but re-generation. Birth by **gift** was a work of God bringing into new life; and, that the beginning of the strength should be shewn to be so, the mother was to shut out all influences that might be supposed to generate strength. It was to be wholly from God. Mere natural powers will never do the work of God. Heaven's work on earth can only be accomplished by influences which the Spirit alone can give. He alone can raise you or me or any of His servants to be what God would have us to be. In saying this, I would not despise natural gifts—a good voice for preaching *e.g.*; such as God gave to Spurgeon—they are valuable, but that alone apart from God's grace could not make a worker for God.

Notice one or two characteristics of "Nazariteship." It calls from even the lawful use of innocent pleasures, for they may be the means of unfitting for God's service. "Eat no unclean thing," *i.e.*, those forbidden by the ceremonial law. Samson must shew he was not guided by self-will but by the will of God. He was to give God's service precedence of all else and natural relations be set aside. One rule was that his hair was to grow, for it was the type of the life that comes out of the heart and gives forth among men. If the Nazarite term were completed without flaw, then his hair might be burnt **with** sacrifice—not **as** sacrifice—for none can ever get beyond the words "Nothing in my hand I bring." We have nothing in ourselves that is worthy, but God is pleased to accept of our services and to regard them as "an odour of a sweet smell; acceptable; well-pleasing to Him through Jesus Christ." Poor Samson got so entangled in folly, he let his Nazarite hair get into the mud, when sin and treachery and force prevailed against him!

8. In Samson's parents we have a beautiful pair. They were of this evil tribe but they seem to have been a man and woman of Faith and had holy thoughts. They also had a right estimate of sacrifice and the relation of man to God and saw the proper thing to do; for we cannot suppose they meant to sacrifice to the Angel as a **man.** What a delightful and natural way too they yielded to God when called by Him! What a word for Christian parents here! Though what was promised was against nature, there was not a doubt but they asked how to deal with the wondrous child destined for a special work. They did not say "The Lord will look after him;" but recognised that He would work **through them.**

12. As much as to say "Now we accept Thy Word." They

ask no sign. They know all they desire shall come to pass in due time, though manifesting much anxiety as to how, in their felt weakness, they might be equal to this task. There is a responsibility in training children God has given. Though their destiny is not ours to determine, it is as dear to us as our own and our hearts echo Abram's prayer "Oh! that Ishmael might live before Thee." Also we have to arrange the child's life—to say what he shall be taught, what shall be seen and heard by him—and shall we not also say "Teach **us** (*v.* 8)." There is great difference in children. In some on whom most care is bestowed, the crooked twist will come out. It is a difficult, solemn, painful question. Still have **we** to say with Jacob—"I have waited for Thy salvation." Try Manoah-like, to say "How shall we order this child?" and so carry out that training, that God may be able to say of you as of Abraham "I know him that he will command his children and his house after him." Some of us are too severe; some too lax; some too lazy; some too anxious. The dangers are many. It rests on us to lead every inch of the way we can; to take away every stumbling-block; and what honour can be greater than ordering a child for God? It is well to remember that God has heard prayers that are not answered yet. The answer will come, though we may not live to see it. There is no promise that we shall **see** our prayers answered, but we know an answer will come though it may be in a way that we do not expect and perhaps not until after we are gone, so that we may have to say "I have waited for Thy Salvation."

15–24. Note two branches of Truth. Communion with God must be based on Sacrifice. When Manoah proposed "a kid" for his visitor, there was evidently an intimation that it was as an "offering;" and if his intention were to offer a "sacrifice," it must be to Jehovah. When on earth Christ did not reject the worship of men, but here He takes only the character of messenger or angel. Manoah, doubtless guided, offers the kid as a Burnt-offering on the rock as an altar, and when the smoke of the sacrifice went up to heaven the Angel also ascended unconsumed in the flame; a scene similar to that which Moses saw at the Burning Bush. This was evidently the second Person in the Godhead; for God did reveal Himself in some **partial** manner by occasional communion with His servants before the Incarnation, through One bearing the semblance of a man and of an angel. Communion then is based on Sacrifice. Sacrifice and worship have the closest relation and are connected. The Romish Church says the highest act of worship is the Eucharist! Under this false statement lies a truth, for the highest act of worship is when we lean our hand on the Divine Sacrifice and thus lay hold on God. Christ gives Himself back to us to be the food of our souls; but the Lord's Supper distinguishes between the creature of His hand and Himself. The Eucharist or Transubstantiation is a travesty of the Truth, and what are the effects of it as used by the Enemy to get hold of men's souls? We see one effect in the manner Sunday is turned into a day of worldly pleasure. Early communion and the rest of the day spent in amusement, boating, etc. The old-fashioned Sunday has died out. . . . But, having been justified by faith let us have peace with God; or, in Old Testament language "Let us feed on the Peace Sacrifice;" seeing Christ as our Peace thus given in Sacrifice.

Manoah and his wife saw a little of the truth that they would be linked with God through the "sacrifice" on this Altar. The flame burnt and they were not consumed, for the Lord came not to destroy but to commune with them. The flame ascended to heaven and the Angel in it; manifesting He was no being of earth or time, for He was sinless, therefore the flame could not consume Him. Scripture does not say Elijah went to Heaven in a chariot of fire but that it **went with him** or he would have been consumed. But though he appeared on the Mount of Transfiguration, he was a being of mortality not of resurrection. He will be sent before Christ returns in glory and will die (*Rev. xi.*); but the laws of mortality have not been reversed for him. Christ is the "first fruits" and there could be no resurrection before His. The Incarnation is the ground of man's peace with God. Jesus was God upon earth! A wonderful truth which we cannot understand. God in Christ! One with the Father! Not merely His delegate but God Himself! He was the Image of God because as truly God as the Father and the Spirit are God. Thus we see the communion of this believing pair with God was the display to us of that which is possible now and which will be enlarged to the full by and by. That "secret" "wonderful" Name (*v.* 18) will be so communicated to us, that we shall know It, and see the Prince of Life! Why? Because there has been for us that Sacrifice of which Manoah's was a type.

25. We here learn that this man's service was in no sense self-chosen. Let us remember this for ourselves. Every servant of God is "called" to service by God and what they do is in virtue of that "call," though all are not called to the same service. Samson is not Gideon; nor is Gideon Barak but all are God's servants to do the work He has given them. And there is One Who has said "Leave all and follow Me" *i.e.*, all earthly claims. His servants are first His people. Grace saves; then grace is needed to know the work that has to be done as servants: not because of any innate cleverness but because of God's enablings to do the work to which He calls.

Ch. XIV. **Samson's failures.** The tribe of Dan was on the border of the Philistines and those who so dwelt were always in greatest danger of mixing in unholy friendships which were forbidden. The men of Dan did mingle with the Philistines, thus Samson's marriage with one does not seem to have been an uncommon thing, much as his godly parents may have objected to it. His name too may have arisen from the same cause,—it being the same word in Hebrew as "sun,"—as if from some connection with the idolatrous worship of the Sun. We cannot tell if this were so, but we must realise these associations if we would understand the evils and snares in his life. Samson's story is one of Divine Grace. He was probably made conscious that the Spirit of God was moving in him at times, so as to endue him with strength beyond nature. How, we cannot say. Had it not been so, he would not have dared to touch the lion; but that incident taught him how God had endued him with supernatural strength for the work which was committed to him. Men picture him of enormous size; of great muscle and strength naturally; but he was clearly not of gigantic stature or sinew, and probably the reference in Heb. xi. 34 "out of weakness made strong" is to him, or the Philistines would not have needed to ask where his strength lay. So with God's servants now. He does not give them strength wholesale to do as they like, but gives it according to their day. The "martyr's" strength comes when the emergency and need arise. No confessor for Christ should dare to say "I will remain firm as a rock"—see e.g. Cranmer—for in our little work the same strength is available for our need. Grace to live and grace to die with—timely grace—"grace to help in time of need."

In the causes of Samson's failures notice first is a "love of the world." But remember, that which was "the world" to him is not what it is to us. Circumstances are arranged so around us as to present different aspects to each individual. Samson's temptations may not have been ours, and though we might not have fallen into his snare, Satan is so crafty, that he will have a Timnath for each of us if we attempt to stand in our own strength. We should pray to be shewn what the world is to us, and seek grace to turn from it. The "lust of the eye" and the "pride of life" are things of the world and not of God. Anything that shuts God out, **that** is the world. Samson should never have gone to Timnath. He was a Nazarite and as far as we can tell from the history, he did not break his vow; but feeling he was a separated man, he may have concluded he was in no danger, though it was as necessary for him to keep from connection with the Philistines and from Delilah as from wine. Thus in Ritualism, much stress is laid on Lenten fasts; fish on Fridays, etc.; but this is followed by balls, etc., etc., when Lent is over! To have the outside right without the inside is useless. Samson's outrage on parental authority was a gross evil and contrary to the Jews even now; for parental authority is peculiarly exercised among them. It is an ordinance instituted by God's providence. It is He Who has said "Children, obey your parents;" but in these days, children imagine they are wiser than their parents. But God's law cannot be thrust aside with impunity and this command being so gainsayed is a proof that the world is going on rapidly to the coming Antichristian apostasy.

CH. XIV., XV., XVI. **Four incidents in the life of Samson which are illustrations** (not types) **of the work of Christ.** The first is in ch. xiv. 5–14—slaying the lion, and his riddle—"Out of the eater came forth meat and out of the strong sweetness." Possibly he only meant to make a conundrum or play upon words; but when we examine it, it suggests to us higher thoughts; even of a mightier One than Samson being strengthened to accomplish God's purposes, Who came forth to interpose against God's enemy and man's enemy—Satan. Scripture shews it was the personal Devil who opposed Jesus and who has gained all he has by usurpation by God's permission; for he used those remarkable words respecting his power in the world—"That is delivered unto me and to whomsoever I will I give it!" He also had power over Death and Christ needed to be rescued from that! This explains Gen. iii. 15 for Satan roared in lion-like fury against the Holy One (*see Ps. xxii.*). That mysterious conflict with the powers of darkness was "the hour of Satan." So think of the Mighty One meeting the man-slayer—him, in whose cruel hand the world still lies—and remember our mighty Samson has conquered him and that all our sweetest thoughts of Christ are connected with His Cross. What is sweeter to us than redemption in Christ Jesus, in which in its completeness and adequacy all the requirements of God and needs of man have been met. "Through death, Jesus destroyed (*i.e.*, nullified) him that had the power of death." The legal power was taken from Satan. Thus "out of the strong came forth sweetness." Perhaps while Jesus lay in the grave the hosts of hell thought Christ's work had failed. But the bitterness of the death of Jesus is the sweetness of life to believers!

The second incident is in ch. xv. 9–20. In Samson's first conflict with the Philistines it was so arranged that his victory over them was "of the Lord." The "men of Judah" (pitiful friends they were to him) said "We are come to bind thee and deliver thee to the Philistines," and all he answered was "Swear not to kill me yourselves." In other words "As long as **you** don't kill me, I can deal with the rest;" as if he did not count on divine strength being given against Judah, only against the Philistines. And in one moment God's power came upon him with absolutely supernatural strength and not a moment too soon; as it is said "As thy day, so shall thy strength be," *i.e.*, when the need ariseth strength is given. The lesson from this is, that when our great Deliverer came, His method was contrary to all the conceptions of man. Just as Samson won deliverance with merely "the jawbone of an ass," so from 1 Cor. i. 27 we learn what despised means God often uses to be "the power of God unto salvation;" *viz.*, "the foolishness of preaching." The Jews looked for a Monarch of **power** to deliver them, because they were looking for worldly establishment in the earth. They were not seeking forgiveness but deliverance from the Romans; so "Christ crucified" was a "stumbling block" to Israel, inspiring them with contempt; scornfully saying "He trusted in God, etc.," and this contempt was carried on even in Corinth among the worldly Jews!

It was in this light that the Government regarded the work of the Baptist missionaries in India; and now they only look upon them as a means of opening up the way for trade, commerce, etc. And in our land, announcement is found on many Churches of "bright services, etc.," but not of the Gospel being preached—that being still but as "a jawbone" in men's sight—yet, if it be guided by God it is still a "power of God unto Salvation." To the Greeks it was "foolishness;" they looked for a learned philosopher and were willing to listen up to a certain point; but when it came to the fact of an **atoning death** making men holy, they regarded it as an absurdity; yet this "foolish thing" of God succeeds. Would there were more true Christians in the world who would faithfully use this weapon! Men must admit that Christ was the only perfect Man the world ever saw, and the best lives the world has ever seen are those of men who have followed Him, much as they have failed. So God does work by what men call "foolishness." He does not need to be helped out with the spear of modern fashion. Read Whitfield's sermons. Nothing could be simpler. They were not striking, but they were much used of God and the worst of men who listened to them trembled.

The third incident in Samson's life was carrying away the gates of Gaza (*ch. xvi.* 1–3)! The fourth was pulling down the house of Dagon upon himself and the Philistines (*v.* 21–31)! The first is an illustration of the work of Christ over the power of death on the **bodies** of His people. He said to Peter "The gates of hell shall not prevail against My Church," and Samson did not unlock the gates of Gaza! He took up the posts with the gates! A grim answer to the taunts of his enemies who found both the gates and Samson gone! Thus when Christ descended into the grave, He made Death powerless against His people, because its right and title against them had been satisfied; so to the saints it is but "sleep." The second death shews there is a grave for the soul as there is for the body; but the believer can say as he sinks in death and finds himself in the arms of Jesus, "O death, where is thy victory?" Samson slew more in his death than in his life, thus he gained **his** supreme victory in death!

In the Word of God the biographies of men are so told as to prove their truth. God shews us man at his best and at his worst. The first page of Samson's history is the best and the last page the worst, when, as captive to the Philistines, he desired to bring down the house of their god on them! His act must be called suicide, his idea being that the Philistines were more *his* enemies than God's and one motive, revenge for the loss of his eyes. So, to speak of a Type here would bring us into great difficulty. His history changes to gloom and sets in evil. This is not as it should be with the servant of God. It may be said of some Christians that they live too long, so that the last part of their life seems an undoing of the first. Length of days is not always increase of grace, and I should like to say to the young, that as I look back over my early days I see much I would like to have done and the opportunity is gone; but yours are beginning. May they be so given to God as to be all days of usefulness and so spent, as to be the promise of more and more grace. As St. Peter says "Give diligence to make your calling and election sure" *i.e.*, So live, that others may have no doubt of your condition eternally. May every year the proof be clearer that you are God's children.

Ch. XVI. Spiritual Lessons from the life of Samson. The first of these is connected with his going down to Gaza. Ver. 1 just conveys the intelligence of this journey, and yet when we think to what that journey led, this short phrase is full of meaning and suggests how readily we may fall into a tide of evil if careless as to the circumstances which lead to it. Idle curiosity appears to have been Samson's reason or may be the same evil passions which moved him to go to Timnath. Had he never gone to Gaza he would not have fallen into the consequent evil there and at Sorek (*xvi.* 4). In all Christians' lives there are Gazas into which they may go if they make self-will the motive of action and the guide of life without the counsel of God. Believers often begin by desiring something and end by thinking it right. Life is like a chain of links; each circumstance in our lives being linked into the next. Children of God, take heed of journeys to Gaza in your souls. Make sure that the terminus is right in God's sight.

Again at Lehi (*xv.* 14). Having been bound by the men of Judah, Samson, by the Spirit of the Lord, burst his bonds and then with a jawbone slew 1,000 of his enemies! We look at that "jawbone" in a different light to-day. If God allow us to come into circumstances of evil and temptation not of our own seeking, His promise in such case will avail, that "as thy day thy strength shall be" just as Samson found "the jawbone of an ass" and used it, realising God's strength was behind it. God will never place us in circumstances of difficulty or entanglements out of which He will not find "a way of escape" for us. This thought will give comfort in the hour of difficulty before deliverance comes. The darkness is greatest before the light appears, and at the darkest moment God will surely appear with deliverance. Samson must have trusted God that day. Notice again that the moment the conflict was over, Samson felt the difference between God's strength and his own human weakness. At the moment of victory he felt himself to be dying of thirst, and God at once appeared for his help and caused a spring of water to rush forth to meet his need! Learn from this, God not only meets His servants in their need but also supplies what is necessary for their refreshment; for we have a sympathising High Priest as well as One who can help. The "Man on the Throne" is God, and all things are at His command; so let us use the knowledge of this truth that it may be real to our souls.

Another lesson written large in Samson's life is that he had "a besetting sin." Each of us doubtless has one apart from the general one of "unbelief"—some evil habit of temper—pride, selfishness, sloth, etc. We see instances in the characters of all of whom we have been reading in this Book; and Samson had his. He loved the Philistine women and this reminds us of the warning in 1 John ii. "Love not the world;" for as the Philistine women competed with the women of Israel for Samson's love, so does the world with its voices which speak from Satan compete with God's for the love of His people. Then which of these are **commanding** our hearts? Are we ready to go down to the Philistine world—which is all around and with us—and fall into its perils and attractions? He who **wants** to love the world **will not** see the evil of it. All that is not of the Father is of the world; so if we love what God loves, we shall not be loving the world. The two influences sway us and the scale goes up and down for each. "The world passeth away" (*i.e.* is on the move) and the lust thereof; but he that doeth the will of God abideth for ever." Thus, "doing the will of God" is contrasted with being guided by the desires of the world. The latter has no permanent influence for good, whereas the "doer of God's will" is leading a life which will bear good fruit to God. To be guided by God's will is the very opposite of selfishness.

Dearly belovéd; "Self" gets up in the morning with us; goes along with us all day,—at business, at pleasure, etc.—and is ready to go to bed with us. "Self" is our first thought and is as attractive as Delilah was to Samson, and will be unless God's grace be attractive to our souls. Our hearts are selfish and by the same law of gravitation by which a stone falls to the ground, until the Grace of God enter into our hearts with a "new life" and control us, we cannot be unselfish. For the sanctification of life and soul there must be a pure ideal before us and a power in us of drawing to that ideal. Samson had a depraved ideal—Philistine women—

and to that ideal his unholy passions were attracted. That is the dark side to be shunned; *viz.* the evil things of the world which may attract and charm. But the bright and holy side is, that there is a true ideal like unto which there is no beauty; *viz.* Christ and His holiness, loveliness, unselfishness, devotedness to God. And as Abraham's servant spoke not of himself to Rebecca, but of Isaac and the home and husband awaiting her, so the Holy Spirit testifies of the glories of Christ; as He said "He shall testify of Me."

Lessons from the later life of Samson. If the ground around and between trees and shrubs in a garden were to be opened, what a mass of roots large and small intertwining would be laid bare; and if a portion of the network were examined it would be impossible to say, however careful the search, from which tree or shrub these or those roots came into the mass. Such is not an inapt picture of the human heart. Beneath the surface of our lives lie so many intermingling motives and impulses, flowing from so many currents of thought and feeling, that the most careful analysis would fail in many cases to trace from what causes result and action flow. Sin is a complex problem. The power of temptations is not exhausted in their first assault. The influences of past sins and follies often remain dormant in the soul; and so multiform and varying is the play of impulse in the formation of motives, that none of us could tell precisely, how much of the effects that we feel in our outer and inner lives flow from one or more of the causes to which we might think we could trace them.

One chief object in the biographies of Scripture is to instruct us as to the workings of sin in the soul, by shewing us examples of its effects upon the life. No more instructive but alas, **painfully** instructive example of this can be found than in that of Samson. In his case we see how a man is "drawn away of his own lust and enticed" and are warned, not merely of the deceptive character of sin's workings, but of the cumulative force sin acquires in the soul when progressively indulged in. Samson's snares were the Philistine women. Towards them he was weak while as to the men he was strong. Something of significance appears in the progression of his declension from one case to another. The first, who "pleased him well," stood to Samson rather in the aspect of a passive than an active temptation. She sought him not. The next was one whose evil character was no secret; and Samson, going into the snare, went forward with his eyes open. But in the third case how little did he dream of the net-work of evil that was being cast around him by the influence of his relations with Delilah; meshes soft as silk when first woven, but binding like links of iron when at last they held him fast. The green withes and new ropes wherewith the Philistines sought to bind him were not so strong as the evil charms of the woman who lured him to his fall. He could break the one, but he little realised the strength of the glamour of her deception. Thus it is with sin. It is not so much the weight of temptation at the first onset that we have to fear as its power to deceive and enslave the soul. Not so much the binding power of the first links sin casts around us, as its ever growing cumulative power to harden and delude. So the first lesson is the power of sin upon the soul illustrated in three points.

First. **The attractive power of sin.** It has power over us in virtue of the fact that our nature itself is evil. The nature of the attraction of the magnet over the needle is in the nature of their respective substances. If iron were not iron it would not cleave to the magnet. The needle of the compass turns to the Pole because there is a physical bias inclining it to the north. Sin is no accident in the nature of humanity; it has in humanity its abiding home. It is indeed oneself, and only he who has experienced the regenerating of the Holy Ghost forming a new nature within the soul can speak of any aspect of his being which is not permeated by sin. Even then he has to say "I know that in my flesh dwelleth no good thing." Here then is the secret of sin's attractiveness; but we learn also another aspect of special importance, *viz.* its delusiveness (*see Heb. iii.* 13); and is not sin delusion? Does it ever present itself or God or anything in its true light? Does it not call that pleasure which is not pleasure and paint happiness in false colours, for it leads to everlasting woe. Alas! many a man has found out even in this world the delusiveness of sin, and in Samson's life its work is solemnly depicted.

Second. **The seductiveness of sin.** To seduce is to draw away; and sin draws aside the soul to itself away from God "in Whose favour is life." How little Samson realised when he went after the seductions of sin that every step he took into the land of the Philistines was a step away from God! He may have thought God would go with him; that he might find God in prayer and realise His strength in the land of the Philistines when he turned away from the land of Israel; but the path was one of danger and so he found to his cost! Brethren, let us dwell in the land of God's presence. Let us keep ourselves in the love of God, *i.e.* within the circle that the love of God has drawn around us. Let us fear to take one step into doubtful paths lest we should find *there* influences of evil that attract and delude our souls into snares we may not recognise, until a point of practical failure has been reached from which, as in Samson's case, there is no recovery in this world. Let us remember we *may* lose the usefulness and happiness of our lives, although, through the grace of God, we cannot lose security in Christ; and God **can** keep us if we trust in Him from practical failure as well as from everlasting ruin; from stumbling as well as from falling.

Third. Notice **the secret of Samson's fall.** The most singular feature of his history was his Nazariteship—the symbol of separation to God and devotedness to His service—but what a remarkable contrast between that and his proneness to certain forms of evil in his natural character! It would seem as though God distinguished between Samson the Nazarite and Samson when he lost his Nazarite character, for the purpose of teaching us holy lessons respecting the secrets of spiritual success. One thing is certain. So long as he maintained his Nazariteship *i.e.*, as long as his hair remained intact,—the symbol of inviolate consecration to the service of God—God acknowledged him. But when that hair was shorn, God left him; and it was probably to emphasize this lesson that we find in Samson's case that all his victories were wrought single-handed, as if to distinguish God's willingness to work by an **individual** alone so long as he filled a Nazarite relationship. As we ponder his fall, may we not be reminded of the words "The secret of the Lord is with them that fear Him" and this secret granted to Samson was known to none till *he* revealed it; but alas! when he ceased to fear God and allowed sin to usurp authority over his heart, he betrayed it himself into the hand of the enemy! How instructive are the thoughts this suggests! We too are Nazarites. God has made known the secret of an invincible strength. With us it remains to hold and use that secret as our own; and while we thus walk in the power of the Holy Ghost, realising that "greater is He that is in us than he that is in the world," spiritual success is assured.

There are then three leading thoughts connected with the typical position of Nazariteship. Separation from earthly springs of impulses and motives. The entire devotion of all the energies of life to God *and* God's acceptance of the consecration and its fruits. The Nazarite was to drink no wine; as if to signify that his impulses and strength were not those sustained by nature but by God. His hair was to grow uncut; as if to signify that all the energy flowing from him was to be kept entirely for the Lord. And at the termination of the period of his Nazarite vow, if the conditions of Nazariteship had been preserved, he was to shave himself and consume that hair in the fire under the sacrifice of the Peace offerings; offering it to God as the emblem of an unsoiled and perfect consecration along with the atoning merit of the offering with which it was consumed; a beautiful picture of Christian walk and service. But alas! how terrible the lesson as to this Samson's history supplies! A Nazarite who had lost his Nazariteship when he lost his locks; a man devoted to the service of God from whom the God Whom he had served was departed; a man whose strength stood allied with his consecration but who, when that was lost, was as weak as water in the hands of his foes and died dishonoured in their midst! May we learn to say of this instruction "Moreover by these is Thy servant warned."

Again, a Christian backsliding from God may practically become the servant of sin and do the world's worst work! When Samson was blinded he was physically helpless, and as the Lord had departed from him he became weak as other men; so the Philistines bound him in fetters and made him grind in the prison house. Thus three solemn lessons present themselves. That departure from God entails spiritual blindness; spiritual weakness; spiritual bondage; and it is possible for a Christian so to fall a prey to the deceitfulness of sin, that all these evils may come upon him! It is a terrible thing that spiritual blindness may supervene on spiritual declension, so that at last a man may come to see wrongly and to feel wrongly about the realities of the spiritual life; to make such mistakes as *he* might make, who sees not at all or whose sight is so defective as to deprive him of the power of rightly discriminating the objects of his view. A backsliding Christian is described in 2 Peter i. 9 as "blind" *i.e.* shortsighted; not the blindness of the unregenerate but one whose spiritual sight had become impaired by slothfulness, declension, sin; and in whom there has been none of the **developments** of the "graces" mentioned in the context.

We see then we cannot stand still in the Divine life. We **must** either go forward—which is the law of that "life—"or backwards from any point of blessing we have reached; a solemn thought for every heart. Our will must work with God's will. Our desires must flow in accord with His Law. We must seek to "work out" into practical detail as He "works in us to will and to do of His good pleasure" if there is to be development and fruitfulness and advance; or blindness and feebleness will come! Thus it was with the church in Laodicea, and her great need was that her eyes be anointed with eye salve to see heavenly facts aright.

Sin also entails spiritual weakness. As in natural things, strength increases by exercise, so in the spiritual sphere. The energies of the "new man" require development; and in order to give this the Holy Spirit dwells within, strengthening our infirmity; that as by grace we make use of grace, so does the strength of grace practically increase; for "To him that hath shall more be given." The question for us is, do we use the help and spiritual food God appoints for us? Are our souls active; filled with holy energy; anxious to press on to that which is before us? If not, our strength will be sure to fail, and as it fails, we may be overcome of evil that can only be successfully resisted in the strength which God giveth to those that realise they have none of their own.

Then spiritual blindness leads to spiritual slavery. If we are not servants of God, we shall be of Sin in some sense; and if God be not the Master Whom we serve, we may be sure that for the time being we shall be servants of evil, like Samson in the prison house of the Philistines. **For them** he ground! **For them** he made sport! Thus he **wrought** both for the nourishment of the world's evil and for the increase of its unholy joy!! How awful to think a Christian may work the work an ungodly world wants done and become in that humiliation the theme of their mirth; the butt of their scorn! Yet is it not so all around? Are not worldly Christians doing the world's work of corrupting the Church; the Truth; the service of God? Is it not in some cases men who truly belong to God who, by unholy relationships with the world, unholy concessions to the world's principles and ways, really *do* the work of the world **for it**, and sometimes more effectually than the world could do it itself? Alas! it is often so; but brethren, from **such slavery** may God keep us and give us grace to see aright the influences and agencies of evil around: to render Him a service of honour and not become "servants to sin."

Notice God's faithfulness to His erring servant. When Samson was in his deepest sorrow and humiliation—fallen to the lowest point of disgrace—God was willing to magnify His grace by interposing on His servant's behalf! What an illustration of 2 Tim. ii. 12, "If we deny Him, yet He abideth faithful." Samson had practically denied God. He had betrayed God's secret to His enemies; lost his Nazarite separation; and God had practically denied him by departing from him and giving him into the hands of the Philistines! But God "cannot deny Himself," *i.e.*, though He can give up the **practical** relation to His people which He has made dependent on their obedience, He cannot give up the relation of Grace which He has taken towards them in **Christ**; and He encourages us to make use of this fact; building upon His Grace when we cannot build upon our own response to that Grace.

Poor Samson in all his blindness had a glimpse of this when he cried, "Remember me, O Lord, and strengthen me I pray, only this once." Jehoshaphat also, when allied with unholy Ahab and cried out (surely in prayer) in supreme danger—his life imperilled in a war that he was certainly not sent on by God—yet God in undeserved Grace heard and answered him. Moses too, is an example of this. Before Israel he dishonoured God and before Israel God set him aside from the honoured position of being their leader into Canaan. But this did not touch the principle of Grace given " for Christ's sake ; " for he stood by his Redeemer's side on the Mount in glory ! There are dark moments in the life of all of us when we realise our unlikeness to our Lord, and our own practical unfitness to stand in relationship to Him. Let us remember at such times the God of Samson.

> "While all things change, He changes not,
> He ne'er forgets tho' oft forgot!
> His love's unchangeably the same,
> And as enduring as His Name."

In the last place let us consider the principle of " Selfishness "—the root of all unrighteousness. Among the many motives that urged Samson to his last great act, " selfishness " alas, played a leading part. The words " that I may be avenged upon the Philistines " shew that the desire for the gratification of revenge was perhaps the strongest. He was ready to give his own life if only he could have his own way in involving them in a larger destruction ; a heavier calamity than he had ever brought on them before ! Thus Samson suffered for Self. The principle even of his work of suffering was after all " self-pleasing ! " A hideous picture indeed ; a humbling picture ; and yet, could we but see it, a picture that suggests much of the inveterate selfishness of our own hearts. It is the very principle of our fallen nature ; the root of our sin ; but that which distinguished Christ from us His unworthy servants and followers is told in these simple words " He pleased not Himself ! " In proportion as we are delivered from the bondage of Selfishness and guided by holy motives to please God, shall we find deliverance from all that disfigures, embitters and dishonours our service to bear His yoke and learn of Him and find rest to our souls.

In conclusion, let us read the history of Samson as teaching us that no gift of God is to be used independently of Himself :

no strength can make us strong unless the strong One be with us and we with Him.

CH. XVII. It is difficult to tell the position of the latter chapters in Judges. There is nothing to indicate their chronological order. They rather appear to be an appendix to the Book. Notice the phrase twice repeated. "There was no king in Israel." What a rough, half-pagan state is here described; for between each Judge there was no controlling power; so we have examples of **perverted light**; **perverted morals**; and **perverted worship**!

This people, whether of Judah, Levi, Dan or Ephraim, all possessed the privileges of the Israel of God, *viz.*, adoption, glory, covenants, the Law, the promises; and yet they are here found ignorant of the spiritual nature of their God and approximating their worship of Him to that of the heathen's gross ideas of worship and morality! *e.g.*, Micah, though dwelling at Mount Ephraim, not far from the centre of light at Shiloh, being guilty of theft and only returning the money to his mother when he began to fear the curse she had pronounced against the thief. He had also a house of idols—a species of Pantheon—full of gods!

The image here described represented Jehovah and was to be placed in the house with the idols Milcom, Baalim, etc.! shewing the mixed up state of his mind and of his religion which he had arrived at by **perverted light.** God had given Israel light and forbidden the representation of Himself by an image; but little by little the thought became idealised, and men came to think God must be like a man. Thus, Roman Catholics say they worship the Being represented by an image and like Micah found their arguments on **perverted** light. The moment we refuse to assent to God's commands we get on an ice-slope, as Israel when they began to mingle the Name of God with degraded human idols and bargained with conscience in mixing with the heathen nations round. Thus the light they had was perverted and became darkness! Christendom alas! has done the same and is doing it still in this country where Light has shone! Many in this land are going back to idolatry from much greater light; so let us not read of Micah with censoriousness, for our light perverted may lead to evil as great as his. The moment we put anything in God's place or in that of His principles, we may fall into the same condition of darkness.

Then as to **perverted morals.** Micah had the two tables of the Law. He knew the eighth command and yet he stole his widowed mother's money—a mean sin. This grown-up man stole his mother's capital, and with mean selfishness still guiding his soul, confessed that he took it but that fear of her curse compelled him to return it. Thus perverted principles yield immoral actions. What a man believes guides him to what he does. There are no good morals without faith in right principles: even the world admits there is no morality like to that of the Decalogue and the Sermon on the Mount. But men won't be tied down to rules; some even say there is no distinction between right and wrong, and so are becoming "like fishes of the sea with no ruler over them," till in the end they will welcome the Antichrist who will control them. By books, speeches, etc., the minds of men and foundations of morality are being unsettled. We should seek to have high ideals. Morality won't rise higher than the morality which is the law of conduct.

We have also here an example of **perverted religion.** Here is an irreligious, unkind, disobedient, mean thief violating also the fifth command; yet he could not get on without some form of religion (*v.* 5)! He was one who meant to make the best of both worlds. It was a selfish religion—a priest and an image to himself. Such perverted religion marks us. "Making one's peace with God" is a degrading phrase. There is no thought of repentance in it, but merely an anxiety to see how one's debt to God can be cleared off and conscience kept quiet apart from that religion which reminds that God is a Spirit. External religion is not objected to, but God was not honoured by Micah's religion, though with his god and his Levite he looked a religious man. True religion is nothing unless in the heart, and does not consist in seeing what we can give to God but in seeking blessing from Him. He Who sees the heart wants the heart; not the life without the heart.

CH. XVIII. In bringing before you the spiritual lessons of this chapter I wish to awaken in you a deeper interest in and respect for Old Testament Scriptures, for " all Scripture is given by inspiration of God and is profitable, that the man of God may be perfect." Therefore, if parts are left out, the rest cannot do the work of the whole. We have seventeen chapters, the histories of which did not grow brighter but on the contrary, increasingly dark and sad. This may possibly be owing to the fact stated four times in these later chapters as if to emphasize its significance —" There was no king in Israel ; everyone did that which was right in his own eyes ! " Israel had been a theocracy. *Then* a State church was right, for their King was God. But when Divine worship languished, the Divine laws of morality languished also. No religion ; no morals. If men lose faith in God, they begin to do what is right in their own eyes, a condition we are fast coming to in Christendom through a decadence of Faith.

Let us see how it came to be that the tribe of Dan was in the position in which we here find it which was the origin of all this evil. When Israel first came into Canaan, a part of the south-west corner was apportioned to Dan, but being deficient in energy, they never properly took possession by driving out the Amorites ; thus its history begins with mistake and failure, each one leading on to other mistakes and failures, for the children of Dan without a home were always in a constrained inconvenient position, and here we find them doing a strange thing ; *viz.*, turning away from their inheritance in the south and instead of expelling the Amorites there, making a pilgrimage to the north to take up a tract on the outskirts of Canaan ; not accepting God's place and plan for them but marking out a self-chosen one in self will ! Their spiritual representatives have not died out in these later days and God's people have been defeated when they should have won a victory through doing the same. But the energy of selfwill is the very opposite of Christ's command " to take His yoke and learn of Him " and the best things for those who reject God's yoke is to have their self-will crossed.

Second lesson. Men, whose hearts are far from God,

are often glad to seek sanction from Him for their own plans. Conscience lingers long in a man before it dies, and under the voice of conscience, men seek to make some sort of bargain with God and are thus guided by superstition. Thus these Danites were unwilling to go against the people of Laish without first obtaining the aid of this priest of Micah, who, though he knew it to be a wrong proceeding, consented, for it suited himself and them; and this sort of thing is not worn out in the Christianity of the present day.

Lesson three is very striking; *viz.*, the peculiar seductiveness of idolatry, which constrained Paul to write as he did to the Corinthians (*ch. x.*). He knew there was Satanic influence in it leading them to imagine it is nothing; but it *is* something; for the principle connected with it of giving allegiance to other than God comes in, saying "God is far off, here is something near;" and it is this makes it so seductive. Yet it was for *this* that God provided the Incarnation, that He might be known through Jesus. The Danites found comfort in these graven images and the teraphim—the heavy for their house, the smaller to carry about—and let *us* not think we are above the seductiveness of these things, but remember John's warning "Little children, keep yourselves from idols." There are ten thousand things ready to draw hearts away from God. Beware of them, and know it is only by the power of the Holy Spirit realising Christ's presence in the soul (not in the sacraments or in peals of the organ or dim religious lights) that there is comfort and safety. God must be worshipped in spirit.

Lesson four is, that immorality springs out of idolatry, while at the same time seeking to shelter itself under cover of religiousness. This is a day of blatant infidelity—men saying they have nothing to do with God but will do as they like! Yet conscience will speak, though may be occasionally only and cannot wholly be ignored until it becomes seared. There are those who run after sin; men whose god is "getting on" and who in their pursuit of money will cheat etc. under the ægis of religion, for conscience makes them go to early communions and once in the day to church; yet all the while comforting themselves they are under the shelter of God, just as the Danites cherished idolatry as a sop to their evil.

Let us beware of making religion a cover for our sin, imagining it brings us into relation to God and that consequently our evil cannot be so very bad. God will have the first place in our hearts or none. Not Christ and the Belial of cupidity, worldliness and false profession, for Christ and Belial cannot dwell in the same heart.

Lesson five is the picture of a worldly ministry. False priests and false religion make a false people and a false people make false prophets. The children of Dan thought the false priest could bless their ways and he was willing to take that false place, thus helping them to be more wicked. That idol house may have been æsthetically and ecclesiastically faultless but it was an abomination to God, and this false priest was willing to steal the idols for the Danites' use, and so sinking to the level of the people to whom he ministered professedly for God! Thus, Christendom of to-day does not find its ministers reproving evil in the people; but mark, where there is not personal holiness there can be no personal relation with God. McCheyne's influence was not so much in his sermons as in the holiness of his life. True holiness of heart is the secret of power. "Without holiness no man shall see the Lord."

30. Then notice the power of idolatry to keep its stand when once established. The idolatrous priesthood continued in this false priest's family till the captivity, so that the tribe of Dan was the home of idolatry through the reigns of David, Solomon and their successors; and was of course the place chosen by Jeroboam to set up one of his calves! It was also within the circle of Israel and Israel's light at Shiloh: thus there were two competing objects for worship; the image in Dan *and* God's ark in Shiloh; and men calling themselves Jews did their best to link them together! Falsehood is never more dangerous or so potent as when linked with Truth; so Paul would have no association with the damsel at Philippi in whom the spirit of Pytho was; and he warns against the wiles of the Devil. What this idolatry could not have done in a heathen land it did do in Israel's! Error dies hard; then let us seek to be shielded from the dangers of these days and to "keep the faith."

Ch. XIX.-XXI. Vengeance v. Vindictiveness.

This book closes with a long history in three chapters, shewing that sin developed more in the tribe of Benjamin than in the others (*xix.* 30). The proofs of this crime were sent to every tribe and the whole nation responded in a remarkable way to the summons to avenge it (*xx.* 1) ; but they were discomfited before Benjamin for two days—though afterwards cutting off all but 600—only their righteous vengeance turned to vindictiveness !

The events of ch. xxi. were carried on close to Shiloh ! No wonder the book ends with the words it does and the history suggests that many similar stories might be told, but that God in mercy withheld them and in the same mercy records this very humbling one ; for "whatsoever things were written aforetime were written for our learning," that we may heed the lessons and avoid the evil. And learn first the unspeakable blessings of good government, which is the basis of all temporal happiness. Had it been exercised in Gibeah, this evil had never been perpetrated, but as it existed not, men of Belial were able to plan and carry out this awful design. Looking on the evils at work in the world around, it might be questioned, **Can** God be ruling on the earth ? Let us be careful to answer such questions rightly. Do not say that God is **governing** now ; for Christ is absent and waiting till His Kingdom has come to **reign** in the earth. But then does not God care for what is going on ? Consider what His relation is to the world now ? 2 Thess. ii. shews that Lawlessness is working peculiarly in the earth at the present time, and would manifest itself as at Gibeah unless restrained by the power of God Who says "Thus far, but no farther."

This is the history of evil in the Bible—God allowing it to go on so far and then bringing on it the judgment it deserves. Not that we may criticize God's ways. He allowed evil to enter Paradise and sin to establish itself there as well as in communities and individuals since. In the Millennium it will be controlled. Satan will be bound and Christ reigning over the earth with a far more real government than that carried out in England. It is a good thing for us that wickedness is measurably controlled, but then it will be so effectually.

The second lesson is the evil of ignorance of Truth where it might be known and the lack of its controlling power. Those were rough times and little Truth known compared with what might have been. Notice, when this stranger came to the city, that contrary to all laws of Oriental society and of Israel, no one offered him hospitality! He was compelled to remain in the street until an old man (not a Benjamite) invited him. The kindness of God as expressed in Lev. xxiii. 22 sufficiently shews how far Benjamin had strayed; and we see a gross character of ungoverned passions flaming out, till the scene presented is like the opening of the mouth of Hell in lessons written large for us. Sin seemed a thing of common occurrence among them, and we must remember that it is our own nature exhibited in them apart from the Grace of God. It is Grace in the hearts of God's children that alone distinguishes London from being as Sodom. God's Truth has built hedges of restriction which save us from such manifestations.

A third lesson is that we should distinguish between vengeance and vindictiveness. The vengeance of the Law is not vindictiveness; and death-warrants may possibly be signed with eyes blinded by tears. There *is* vengeance with God and He will repay; but the modern idea of God is unbalanced with any thoughts of His justice! Holy love must be joined with holy hate. Angels glorify God for His inflexible righteousness. But here we find a human hand put forth to work a vengeance which became ferocious vindictiveness. Observe the difference between men trying to do right but going beyond right; and God, Whose ways are unfailing justice or love.

Now a fourth lesson. When Israel went against Benjamin, they were defeated in an unexpected manner and when they went up to the house of the Lord to enquire it was with feelings of surprise at their rebuffs! They had to learn that no moment is so dangerous to the soul as when dealing with the sin of others, as the hearers of a sermon often see its suitability to their neighbours while their own sin retires into the background in their estimate. Witness the self-righteous Pharisee. So their first lesson was one of repentance. Had they repented of their own sin they would not have gone so far as to kill all the Benjamites. May we have grace to realise that the sin we see in others is merely a reflection of our own, and be enabled to carry out St. Paul's direction in Gal. v. 1 to "restore an erring brother in the spirit of meekness" and not stand on a pinnacle of self-glory.

The other lesson for Israel was that of dependence. There is so much self-dependence instead of leaning wholly upon God that often He cannot help us! Thus we often pray about a matter upon which we have already fully made up our minds! The heart is deceitful and only God knows it. May we seek to have simplicity of dependence, with a hatred of all that He hates and a love for all that He loves.

[NOTE.—*The Judges were chosen from eight of the tribes only, not from Reuben, Simeon, Gad or Asher.*]

THE SOVEREIGN GRACE ADVENT TESTIMONY MANIFESTO

(first published 1919)

To all who believe in our Lord Jesus Christ: A statement of our faith and aims.

Dear Friends,

The Conveners of the Sovereign Grace Advent Testimony Meetings desire to make a clear statement of their position in relation to PROPHETIC TRUTH, in the spirit of love and humility, recognising that we only "know in part".

We adhere to the principle of receiving the Word of God, in its *literal sense*, except where obviously figurative, and in so receiving *Prophetic Truth*, emphasise the fact that this enhances, and does not diminish, experimental enjoyment of the Doctrines of Grace, also so learned.

We, therefore, affectionately lay before you the points on which our testimony is, and will be, united, and invite our readers prayerfully to consider these things, in subjection to the Word of God, and in dependence upon God the Holy Spirit.

1. We receive the doctrines of the FREE AND SOVEREIGN GRACE OF GOD, viz.:
   (a) The Co-Eternity and Co-Equality of the Three Persons in the One Godhead.
   (b) The Full Verbal Inspiration of the Scriptures.
   (c) The Incarnation, Sinlessness, Atonement, Resurrection, and Ascension of God the Son.
   (d) The Substitutional Obedience and Death of the Lord Jesus Christ.
   (e) The Election, Redemption, Regeneration, Justification, Imputation of Christ's Righteousness to, Sanctification, and Final Preservation of all the Saints.
   (f) The Total Depravity of all Mankind, and Entire Perversity from God of the Natural Will.
   (g) The Eternal Life of the Righteous, and the Eternal Punishment of the Wicked.

2. The NEAR APPROACH of the RETURN of the LORD is our confident HOPE.

3. His RETURN we expect as PRE-MILLENNIAL, and following:
   (a) The Apostasy of Israel and Christendom.
   (b) The Ten Kingdom Confederacy.
   (c) The Revival of Babylon and Babylonianism.
   (d) The Reign of Antichrist.
   (e) The Great Tribulation.

4. THE PURPOSES of the Lord's Coming we believe to include:
   (a) The Resurrection of all departed Saints, and the Glorification with them of the Living Saints.
   (b) The Destruction of the Antichrist – the Man of Sin – the Lawless One.
   (c) The Conversion and Restoration of Israel.
   (d) The Gathering Out of His Kingdom of "All things that offend".

(e) The Reign over the Earth, and Manifestation of the Kingdom in Righteousness – Satan being bound and the Earth's groan hushed.
(f) The Judgment of the Great White Throne, at the End of the Millennial Kingdom.
(g) The Creation of the New Heavens and New Earth after the Millennium.

5 The SIGNS which we Discern of His Near Approach are:
(a) The *rapidly* increasing Apostasy of Christendom, with Lawlessness.
(b) Worldwide Testimony of the Gospel, in order to complete the taking out from the Gentiles a People for His Name (Acts 15:14).
(c) The Promotion of Federations, Unions, Leagues, and Alliances, both Ecclesiastical, Social, Commercial, Industrial, National, and International APART FROM *God, His Christ and His Truth.*
(d) The Re-organisation of the Roman Empire, leading to Ten Kingdoms.
(e) The Re-opening of the East, especially of Palestine, Mesopotamia and Egypt, with the Restoration of the Jews to Palestine as their "National Home", in their continued unbelief.
(f) The Fall of absolute Monarchies, and Spread of Constitutional Government. The Rise of Democracy, with Social and Industrial Unrest.

6. SPIRITUAL APPREHENSION of these things, by the teaching of the Holy Spirit, we deem to be ESSENTIAL to a COMPLETE TESTIMONY OF TRUTH, which will lead to practical separation from worldly principles, policies, and pleasures, and to more loyal devotion to the Lord's service.

OUR AIMS are:

1. To hold forth this teaching as and where the Lord Leads.
2. To promote the searching of the Scriptures to "see if these things be so", and to foster such study among young people.
3. To arrange and address any meetings as requested.
4. To recommend lines of study and suitable literature to enquiring correspondents.

THE SOVEREIGN GRACE ADVENT TESTIMONY
seeks to make known the Truth of God by the written message and the spoken message.

The objects are:

1. To teach the near approach of the Lord's return—James 5:8.
2. To hold forth the Truth and to expose and resist error—Jude 3.
3. To note the passing events in the light of "the Scripture of Truth"—2 Peter 1:19.
4. To unfold the Word of God by comparing Scripture with Scripture—Acts 17:11.
5. To encourage missionary endeavour, and all service for the Truth—Acts 1:8.
6. To comfort and strengthen those who seek to stand with the Lord, apart from abounding lawlessness—2 Timothy 2:19.
7. To call for separation from False ecumenism—2 Corinthians 6:14-18.

The written message:

The works of Mr. B. W. Newton, Dr. S. P. Tregelles, Dr. C. Y. Biss, Mr. David Baron, Mr. Herman Newmark, Mr. G. H. Fromow, Pastor James Payne and others are recommended for Bible students.

Also, the magazine "Watching and Waiting" issued regularly.

The spoken word:

Meetings are convened by the Sovereign Grace Advent Testimony for the exposition of the Word of God.

The Sovereign Grace Advent Testimony also has a library of tape recordings on Scriptural subjects, copies of which may be purchased.

For book and tape lists, for "Watching and Waiting", for arrangements for meetings, and for a copy of the Sovereign Grace Advent Testimony manifesto—apply to the secretary, Mr. Stephen A. Toms, 1 Donald Way, Chelmsford, Essex, CM2 9JB.